# Advance Praise for
## *Justice for Black Students: Black Principals Matter*

*"Part autobiographical, part historical, part instructive, and all engaging enjoyment makes this volume a rare treat for the reader who gets to learn closely more about the intellectual giant Kofi Lomotey's culturally rich beginnings, his brilliant research on Black principals, and his compassion for Black children. Captured within is an instructive approach that drove Lomotey to confidently make an impact for Black children by challenging deficit views early in his career and endeavoring to eradicate them by leading schools, even as he studied at Stanford. This thoughtful tome also includes an appreciated presentation of his earliest scholarship with exciting current connections to culturally responsive school leadership, confirming that it should be required reading for ALL educational leadership students. It will be for mine."*

—Mark Gooden, Christian A. Johnson Endeavor Professor in Educational Leadership, Teachers College, Columbia University

*"In* Justice for Black Students: Black Principals Matter, *Kofi Lomotey pulls together a half-century of his research on Black male and female principals. Both his experience as a principal and as a scholar in the field make this book a signal contribution to the literature of a key, but often under-rated, position in the practice of schooling in the U.S."*

—Larry Cuban, Professor Emeritus of Education, Stanford University

*"For a definitive overview of the research on Black principals,* Justice for Black Students: Black Principals Matter *is a must read. Professor Kofi Lomotey examines the research on Black principals conducted over 40 years. Covering the earliest research on the topic through the most contemporary, Lomotey explores several frameworks used to understand Black principals' practice and does not neglect the critical role of gender. Across several chapters, combining empirical research, reviews of the literature, and questions to consider, he takes ⸴ ' ˙ through the research on Black principals. Th*

*against a backdrop of his life experiences. Lomotey does for the scholarship on Black principals what others have done for Black teachers."*

—Michèle Foster, Professor and
Henry Heuser Jr. Endowed Chair, University of Louisville

*"In* Justice for Black Students: Black Principals Matter, *Dr. Lomotey offers a compelling view of how and why culture is important for school leadership. As he pulls together his journey and much of his life's academic works, he masterfully guides readers to consider why school leaders do the work they do, and to ponder their greater purposes and commitments. Researchers and practitioners alike will find useful the discussion questions, and the invitation to think of who they are, and what redeeming qualities they may have, as leaders. This is most palpable in Dr. Lomotey's reflections and synthesis on ethno-humanist school leadership—a concept that he coined, and that would go on to reshape our entire field. What is perhaps most promising is that* Justice for Black Students: Black Principals Matter *offers school leaders, university professors and educators another chance to offer a humanizing and fulfilling educational experience to Black students. It is brilliant and should be read and used widely!"*

—Muhammad A. Khalifa, Professor,
Department of Educational Studies, The Ohio State University

*"In the opening of this much anticipated text, Dr. Lomotey takes us on a journey beginning with the personal by telling his own life story and how it serves as the foundation for his work in the field and frame for this text. This critical choice sets the reader up for a journey into his genius and how he masterfully explicates the contributions of—and need for—the Black principalship in practice and in research. This is an amazing and much needed work for the field of educational leadership and beyond."*

—Judy A. Alston, Director & Professor, Doctoral Program in
Leadership Studies, Ashland University

# JUSTICE FOR BLACK STUDENTS

Copyright © 2022 | Myers Education Press, LLC

Published by Myers Education Press, LLC
P.O. Box 424
Gorham, ME 04038

All rights reserved. No part of this book may be reprinted or reproduced in any form or by any electronic, mechanical, or other means, now known or hereafter invented, including photocopying, recording, and information storage and retrieval, without permission in writing from the publisher.

> **Myers Education Press** is an academic publisher specializing in books, e-books, and digital content in the field of education. All of our books are subjected to a rigorous peer review process and produced in compliance with the standards of the Council on Library and Information Resources.

**Library of Congress Cataloging-in-Publication Data available from Library of Congress.**

13-digit ISBN 978-1-9755-0483-0 (paperback)
13-digit ISBN 978-1-9755-0484-7 (library networkable e-edition)
13-digit ISBN 978-1-9755-0485-4 (consumer e-edition)

Printed in the United States of America.

All first editions printed on acid-free paper that meets the American National Standards Institute Z39-48 standard.

Books published by Myers Education Press may be purchased at special quantity discount rates for groups, workshops, training organizations, and classroom usage. Please call our customer service department at 1-800-232-0223 for details.

Cover design by Teresa Lagrange

Visit us on the web at **www.myersedpress.com** to browse our complete list of titles.

# JUSTICE FOR BLACK STUDENTS

## BLACK PRINCIPALS MATTER

### BY KOFI LOMOTEY

Myers Education Press

Gorham, Maine

# CONTENTS

| | |
|---|---|
| **Acknowledgments** | ix |
| **Foreword**<br>*Sonya Douglass* | xi |
| **Introduction**<br>*Kofi Lomotey* | xv |

### PART ONE: My Early Work

| | |
|---|---|
| 1. My Beginnings: New York City, Oberlin, and Stanford | 1 |
| 2. Black Principals for Black Students: Some Preliminary Observations | 15 |
| 3. African American Principals: Bureaucrat/Administrators and Ethno-Humanists | 29 |

### PART TWO: Issues of Gender

| | |
|---|---|
| 4. Research on the Leadership of Black Women Principals: Implications for Black Students | 55 |
| 5. The Leadership of Black Male Principals: What the Research Tells Us | 95 |

### PART THREE: Justice for Black Students (and People): Ethno-Humanism and Cultural Responsiveness

| | |
|---|---|
| 6. Ethno-Humanism: Extending its Significance | 123 |
| 7. Culturally Responsive Pedagogy/Teaching | 135 |
| 8. Culturally Responsive School Leadership | 145 |
| 9. What Does This All Mean for Black Students (and Black People)? | 157 |
| **Afterword**<br>*Linda C. Tillman* | 175 |
| **About the Author** | 181 |
| **Index** | 183 |

# ACKNOWLEDGMENTS

For nearly 50 years, I have worked at living my life utilizing an African-centered lens to view the world. In that spirit, I choose to articulate my acknowledgements herein in the context of an African-centered value system, the Nguzo Saba. This Kiswahili phrase translates in English to the "Seven Principles of Blackness."

In the mid-1960s, Dr. Maulana Karenga developed a doctrine—a way of life—called "Kawaida," in Kiswahili. The English translation of the word is "tradition." Karenga explored traditional African cultures and extracted selected aspects, arguing that they would be appropriate for Blacks in the US in the 1960s and beyond. He redefined the word "Kawaida" to mean "tradition and reason," acknowledging that he did not blindly select aspects of African cultures, but, instead, chose those that seemed most appropriate.

One aspect of the doctrine of Kawaida is Kwanzaa. Kwanzaa is a seven-day non-heroic African American celebration of life, focused primarily on the youth. It takes place from December 26 through January 1.

A second aspect of the doctrine of Kawaida is the Nguzo Saba. Karenga selected seven principles from African traditional cultures—values that he identified as most appropriate for Blacks in the U.S. today. These values are (1) "umoja" or unity; (2) "kujichagulia" or self-determination; (3) "ujima" or collective work and responsibility; (4) "ujamaa" or cooperative economics; (5) "nia" or purpose; (6) "kuumba" or creativity; and (7) "imani" or faith. Karenga argued that we should practice these values daily throughout the year. In this book, I acknowledge individuals who best exemplify for me the personification of these seven principles.

I first acknowledge my wife of 45 years, Nahuja. The first principle, *umoja* (or unity), speaks to the bond between family, community, nation, and race. Clearly, for me, such unity begins with the bond between Nahuja and me. The first principle also exemplifies my bond with my elder sister, Saundra, who has been there for me since birth!

My daughter, Shawnjua Tien, and my sons, Juba Jabulani and Mbeja Makiri, epitomize *kujichagulia* (self-determination), the second principle. As the principle suggests, they have defined themselves, created for themselves, and spoken for themselves—each in their own way.

The third principle, *ujima* (collective work and responsibility), recalls for me my colleagues at Western Carolina University: Cathy, Robert, Brandi, Darrius, Jess, Emily, and Heidi. For several years, we have exemplified the best in working together to accomplish goals, focusing on equity, ethics, and social justice.

My *Brothers* through the years, best represent the fourth principle, *ujamaa* (cooperative economics). While not blood brothers, down through the years, we have—in unspoken fashion—held the belief that we are *one for all, and all for one.* We would do nearly anything for each other. We love one another: Al, Phil, E. Thomas, Shujaa, Peter, and Amir.

My students over the past 50 years—pre-school through graduate school—represent for me the fifth principle of the Nguzo Saba, *nia* (purpose). What has impressed me most about them, collectively, is that no matter their age, they have always had a purpose in what they have done, and that truism has often motivated each of them to excel.

*Kuumba* (creativity), the sixth principle, goes to none other than our five grandchildren: Ayanna, Isaiah Jelani, Nia Marie, Norah Sanaa, and Zola Therese. Each in their own way, they never fail to display sophisticated examples of very impressive creativity.

Finally, I acknowledge my departed *shero* and heroes with the seventh principle: my mother, Eleanor Kelley; my father, William Kelley; and my "Brother," Hannibal Tirus Afrik. They each displayed unconditional love for me and saw more good in me than I saw in myself. I miss you. The seventh principle, *Imani* (faith): to believe with all our hearts in our people, our parents, our teachers, our leaders, and the righteousness and victory of our struggle.

Again, I salute these amazing individuals who day-in and day-out help me to be the best Kofi Lomotey I can be. Of course, many others have influenced me over the years; I salute them all.

Thank you.

# FOREWORD
## *Sonya Douglass*

In *Justice for Black Students: Black Principals Matter*, Professor Kofi Lomotey gifts us with a long-awaited solo-authored volume inspired by his groundbreaking contributions to the study of Black principals and educational justice for Black students. This book is part memoir and part research synthesis. It is part Lomotey's reflexive collection of previously published work, and is rooted in his experiences as a founder of African-centered schools and as a leading scholar in education. In this volume, Lomotey provides a retrospective examination of how the subfield of Black education leadership began, while underscoring the significance of his research and scholarship over the last 50 years.

Lomotey's educational and academic journey represents a personal and professional path dedicated to improving the educational lives of Black children and Black people worldwide. Shaped by an array of life-transforming experiences that would take him from his birthplace of Harlem, New York, to the campus of Stanford University in Palo Alto, California, for doctoral studies in educational leadership, the book opens with an intimate and moving portrait of Lomotey's early years as an elementary school student attending Public School (PS) 123 in Jamaica, Queens. He recounts the tremendous influence his mother, sister, teachers, university advisors, mentors, and academic environments had on his educational experiences, sense of belonging, and intellectual trajectory. This path would lead Lomotey to Oberlin College and eventually Stanford University to continue his quest to improve educational conditions and life chances for Black people through an African-centered worldview.

xi

This window into Lomotey's personal journey, beginning with his time as a junior high school student experiencing the feeling of being "less than," reminds us how *our belief* in the ability and capacity of our students to learn and succeed is in fact critical to their success. Lomotey's personal and professional life provide a riveting and relevant backdrop for this project, which brings together the various ways the past and future inform our present and the layered considerations and factors that have led us to the need to continue to demand justice for Black students. The study of Black principals, in particular, and the role that they have played and can continue to play in the lives of Black learners invites additional inquiry, argues Professor Lomotey; and what better person than Lomotey to help us understand the origins of this work and where it might take us?

For nearly half a century, Professor Lomotey's scholarship has focused consistently on the liberation of Black people, with special care and attention to the effective education of Black children and youth as part of a larger commitment to justice and equity. In fact, these were his aims in his foundational text, *Going to School: The African-American Experience* (1990), in which he sought to respond to the fact that masses of Black students in the US have not fared well educationally since African people initially arrived on these shores more than 500 years ago.

Lomotey's conceptualizations of the role identities of Black principals (1993) as *ethno-humanists* and *bureaucrat/administrators* are probably most well-known, making their way into subsequent dissertations and other research studies on Black principals and Black education leadership more broadly. As Lomotey explains, in the case of the Black principal, the ethno-humanist role identity—with Black students as a member of their cultural group and community—is concerned with how principals know and understand themselves and their relationship to their society and the world. The bureaucrat/administrator, however, is more concerned with the technical matters of schooling, leading to further racial

FOREWORD xiii

stratification, inequality, and injustice—inhibiting the prospects and possibilities of real education (Shujaa, 1994).

Given the significant growth and expansion of research focused on Black education, Black principals, and the effective education of Black students, it is important not to lose sight of the historic path Lomotey helped establish as one of the first scholars to explore Black principals, and to consider the extent to which the prevailing research literature on the principalship reflected and/or resonated with professionals serving in those roles who identified as Black or African American. This exciting new project brings us full circle from Lomotey's initial line of inquiry, which began with a study of three successful Black elementary school principals who demonstrated the mainstream characteristics of principals in effective schools and so much more. It was their sense of confidence, commitment, and compassion concerning the capacity of their Black students to succeed and their role in facilitating that success that made all the difference, and invites further examination into creating those conditions and levels of support today.

*Justice for Black Students: Black Principals Matter* offers a rich collection of the writings of Professor Kofi Lomotey just in time for a new generation of scholars and practitioners who are seeking more effective ways to advance educational equity and justice in racially and politically polarizing times. By bridging the foundational scholarship on Black principals with new lines of inquiry and application to practice, in this volume, Lomotey provides critical guidance and direction to aspiring education scholars and educators seeking to improve the academic and overall success of Black children and youth through research and leadership practice. We are fortunate to have Professor Lomotey's reflections and contributions presented jointly in this book as both a foundational text and a reminder of the fact that Black students matter, Black principals matter, and Black education research matters.

*Sonya Douglass*
*Teachers College, Columbia University, USA*

# *References*

Lomotey, K. (Ed.). (1990). *Going to school: The African-American experience.* State University of New York Press.

Lomotey, K. (1993). African American principals: Bureaucrat/administrators and ethno-humanists. *Urban Education, 27*(4), 395–412.

Shujaa, M. (Ed.). (1994). *Too much schooling, too little education: A paradox of Black life in white societies.* Africa World Press.

# INTRODUCTION

## *Background*

More than 30 years ago, I posed the question: What's happening to Black students in U.S. public schools? I suggested that scholars and practitioners were focusing too much on the challenges to Black student academic success in school and not enough on the solutions (Lomotey, 1990). I distinguish Black student academic success from Black student (overall) success. Academic success focuses on student performance in the class and on standardized tests. Success refers to academics *and* social, cultural, and spiritual accomplishments or attainment.

Schools in the US—as is the case in other institutions within the US—are influenced significantly by the presence of institutionalized White supremacy: the belief that White people are superior to other people on the planet, coupled with actions that are consistent with—and that reinforce—that belief. The more common phrase is White supremacy. I prefer the term institutionalized White supremacy, which emphasizes the structured, regularized, longstanding, and difficult to disrupt nature of White supremacy. Consistent with institutionalized White supremacy are negative perceptions, low expectations, deficit thinking, and actions that perpetuate or reinforce those beliefs. This is a fundamental dilemma regarding Black student success.

The question that I raised more than 30 years ago is still pregnant with relevance; success in school is still elusive for the masses of Black children—and the focus is more on the problem than on potential solutions. The time to address the issue of Black student success in U.S. public (and private) schools in long overdue. The evidence of this perplexing challenge—brought about because of institutionalized White supremacy—is all around us—for example, the overrepresentation of Black children (1) dropping out of school, (2) in special education, and (3) in vocational education, and the underrepresentation of Black children in (1) gifted and talented programs, (2) high academic tracks, and (3) computer-enhanced classrooms.

In seeking to address the challenge of Black student success, all too often the focus is from a pathological perspective; it is posited that *something is wrong with Black children:* blaming the victim. This pathological analysis is evident when assessing Black student academic success in relation to White students. For example, hypothetically, it might be said that Black eighth-grade students perform three grade levels behind their White counterparts in mathematics. In assessing this dilemma, the more practical and logical approach would be to consider the academic performance of Black children in relation to where they would be *if all things were equal.* Put another way, perhaps educators and others should look at Black student academic success in relation to what it might be if Black people had the life chances to which we are entitled (e.g., economic, educational, health, social, political, and cultural equity). Many have referred to this shortfall as the opportunity gap (Ladson-Billings, 2013). As it relates to education, the lost opportunity includes the absence of (1) quality pre-school experiences, (2) well-resourced schools, (3) well-prepared teachers and administrators, (4) curricula that adequately prepare students for college, and more.

In 1990 I cited four prominent theories that have been posited as explanations for the persistence of limited Black student success (Lomotey, 1990):

- Social deficit (Coleman, 1965; Jencks et al., 1972),
- Genetic deficit (Jensen, 1969; Shockley, 1972),
- Structural inequalities (Bowles & Gintis, 1976; Ogbu, 1978), and
- Cultural differences (Hale-Benson, 1986; Wilson, 1987).

For several decades now, scholars have debunked the first two views (social deficit and genetic deficit). Structural inequalities (the third view) do exist. They are embedded in all institutions in U.S.

INTRODUCTION                                                    xvii

society. We live in a society where people continue to be oppressed based upon the color of their skin and more (e.g., the amount of money they have in the bank, their gender, their sexual orientation, their abledness, their religious preference, their "beauty," their height, and their weight (Lomotey & Aboh, 2009).

Cultural differences are significant because of the impact of power and privilege. Children bring their cultural characteristics with them into classrooms. Nobles (1978) defines power as the capacity of a group to interpret reality and to persuade other groups that it is their reality. Spring (1991) notes that, in addition to being the capacity to *control others*, power also entails the ability of a group to avoid *being controlled* by others. When one group holds power over other groups, and there are cultural differences, the group in power seeks to maintain the status quo and to convince others that the dominant culture is, in fact, their culture—the culture of all the groups. If you can convince a people that the culture of another group (who holds power) is, in fact, their culture, they will begin to act in the interest of the group whose culture they have adopted and will no longer act in their own interest. Allow me to share three brief illustrations of the foisting of one's culture upon other groups.

- A continent is a large body of land surrounded by water. Children in U.S. schools and elsewhere are taught that there are seven continents, and that Europe is a continent. Europe is neither a large body of land, nor is it surrounded by water; it is connected to Asia. The correct name of the continent is Eurasia and there are only six continents.

- Children in classrooms in the US are told that Christopher Columbus discovered the US (in addition to other places in the Americas), when, in fact, Indigenous Peoples, Latinx people, and Africans (Van Sertima, 1976) were in the US and throughout the Americas long before Columbus arrived. How can one discover a place that is already occupied by other peoples?

xviii

- The Mercator projection of the world was developed in the 1500s for sea merchants and has been used ever since in the U.S. and in other parts of the world. This projection distorts the actual relationship between various land masses—usually advantaging White people. For example, the Mercator projection:

  » makes Greenland appear nearly as large as Africa—Greenland can fit in to Africa nearly 14 times; and

  » makes the landmass in the northern hemisphere (where White people predominate) look larger than the landmass in the southern hemisphere (where Black, Latinx, and Indigenous Peoples predominate). In fact, the landmass in the southern hemisphere is 38.6 million square miles, while the landmass in the northern hemisphere is 18.9 million square miles.

These distortions of reality are culture-based. They contribute to the maintenance of the status quo. These are just a few illustrations of a dominant group dictating reality for the dominated group(s). They demonstrate how institutionalized White supremacy operates. They highlight the differences that exist between one group and another. These cultural distinctions are quite significant as they relate to Black student success. What occurs inside the classroom is of critical importance. And the choice of cultural referents employed in imparting the curriculum has implications for the learner. For example, if a teacher is teaching the concept of one plus one equals two, they invariably are teaching other things to the students. This is true based upon what the teacher is wearing, the illustrations they use to illustrate the concept, and much more.

## *Education and Schooling*

Understanding the distinction between schooling and education is important in comprehending this discussion of power and culture.

INTRODUCTION                                                    xix

Black children—like all children—need quality education. What is quality education? I address this question, in part, by sharing Shujaa's (1993) distinction between schooling and education. Schooling extends prevailing power relationships and perpetuates the existing politically controlling cultural orientation. Schooling occurs when one group has power over another group. Through schooling, the culture of a dominant group is imposed upon another. The group that is imposed upon adjusts and adapts in response to contact with the dominant group (Shujaa, 1993).

Education, on the other hand, is learning and internalizing one's own cultural norms. It occurs in informal and formal settings. It provides the wherewithal for members of a group to effectively function within their family, community, and race and to retain the integrity of their own culture in social contexts where unequal power relations exist between cultures (Shujaa, 1993). This conception of education is what I refer to as quality education. It is not simply Black student academic success; it also encompasses social, cultural, and spiritual success for Black students. For Black children, quality education is Black student success. I contend that these aspects are inextricably linked if Black students are to be successful. But who can provide this type of education for Black children?

## Principals

A teacher imparting curricula that acknowledge the culture of the learner is of paramount importance in addressing the challenge of Black student success; children must be able to see themselves in the curriculum (Lomotey, 1989). For this to occur, teachers must acknowledge and respond to the distinct cultures that students bring into the classroom. They must understand, appreciate, respect, and embrace the culture of the learner, including their native tongue, passions, predilections, kinfolk, and everything that characterizes their cultural distinctiveness. The relationship between the teacher and the student is where "the rubber meets the road." This is where the key connections occur.

Principals also play an important role in facilitating curricula that appropriately acknowledge the culture of the learner; they are vital in bringing about Black student success. Specifically, in schools with large numbers of Black children, Black principals can ensure that Black culture is highlighted. This enables Black children to envision themselves being successful and to visualize a link between the curriculum and their lived experiences. This would be a culturally responsive educational experience. Research illustrates that cultural inclusion corelates positively with student success (Khalifa et al., 2016). An important aspect of this critical function of these school leaders is displaying what I have termed the *ethno-humanist* role identity. In this book, I draw on the work that I and others have done over the past nearly 40 years and make the argument as forcefully as I can that we must improve the performance of Black children in schools; we must increase their success levels. One important contributing factor is the presence of Black principals employing culturally responsive school leadership—which I argue includes ethno-humanism.

I am not suggesting that only Black principals can adequately support Black children. There are key components of ethno-humanism, and I—and others—have observed these components in successful Black principals. Because of a shared culture, Black principals can more easily communicate effectively with Black children (Lomotey, 1989). Still, it is possible that other principals can have or develop some, if not all, of these characteristics—through the development of cultural competence. I expand on this idea in discussing the implications for principal preparation programs and professional development later in this book.

In Part III of this book, I discuss the more recent concept of culturally responsive school leadership (CRSL), emphasizing the interconnectedness of ethno-humanism and CRSL and how CRSL—with ethno-humanism as an implicit component—is critically important in addressing the quagmire within which we continue to find Black children in U.S. schools.

INTRODUCTION xxi

## Ethno-Humanism

In 1993, I coined the neologism, ethno-humanism, to describe a particular role identity of successful Black principals (Lomotey, 1993). The construction consists of three parts: commitment, confidence, and compassion. These leaders are committed to the learning of all pupils and are confident in the potential of all children. They display compassion for—and appreciation of—their schoolchildren and for their families and neighborhoods. Moreover,

> These principals are not only concerned with the students progressing from grade to grade; they are also concerned with the individual life chances of their students and with the overall improvement of the status of African-American people. This commitment evolves from the cultural affinity that these individuals feel toward African-American students. (Lomotey, 1993, p. 396)

Ethno-humanism does not just address the academic success of students but, instead, it goes further in addressing the social, cultural, and spiritual well-being of Black students. Academic success is not all that we should be concerned about for Black students. We must be concerned about more comprehensive Black student success.

I was in my early 40s when I coined the term ethno-humanism; yet I vividly recall the influence of Black (educational) leaders displaying this role identity, even in my own childhood—and beyond. In Chapter 1, I share a brief memoir or an exploration of my childhood and early adulthood, delving into the issues and experiences that influenced my development, including the guidance of individuals who displayed a *commitment* to my education, *confidence* in my ability to succeed, and *compassion* for me, my loved ones, and my community—the three C's.

## *About This Book*

Culturally responsive pedagogy/teaching (CRP/T) encompasses instructional strategies that embrace the culture of the learner. I use the term to include what I see as very similar terms, including culturally relevant teaching, culturally relevant pedagogy, culturally responsive teaching, and culturally responsive pedagogy. In each instance, the focus is on designing classrooms and schools wherein the focus is on the culture of the learner.

CRSL is critical in facilitating CRP/T. CRSL is imperative to successfully confront institutionalized White supremacy and address the dilemma of Black student success in U.S. schools. When I refer to CRSL, I am speaking about leadership that embraces the culture of the learner with a focus on equity, ethics, social justice, and the elimination of institutionalized White supremacy. Moreover, I contend that the components of ethno-humanism—confidence, commitment, and compassion—are fundamental and vital components of CRSL. I argue further that it is ludicrous to envision *consistent* CRP/T in any school in the absence of CRSL. The leadership of principals matters.

## Part I

I focus on ethno-humanism beginning in Chapter 1 with a discussion of the first 35 years of my life, wherein I had teachers and mentors who exhibited behaviors toward me that are associated with ethno-humanism. I describe my upbringing—prior to college—and then consider my broad-ranging experiences in undergraduate and graduate school. I talk about my initial interest in Black education as a student at Oberlin College along with my introduction to independent African-centered schools and the Council of Independent Black Institutions (CIBI). From there I describe my experiences in graduate school at Stanford University, where, in my dissertation, I explored the leadership of *successful* Black principals working with

INTRODUCTION                                        xxiii

Black children. Within this discussion, I talk about the individuals who influenced my development—who displayed ethno-humanism toward me.

In Chapter 2, I provide a reprint of the article that I wrote (Lomotey, 1987) in which I summarize my first study, from 1985, of Black principals in schools with academically successful Black students. The publication of this article in 1987 preceded my coining of the term ethno-humanism (in 1993), but the characteristics of this role identity (confidence, commitment, and compassion) are vividly described and illustrated in this 1987 work. This reflects the beginning of my publishing on Black principals (excepting my 1985 dissertation) and was one of the earliest studies published on this topic.

In 1993, I published an article in *Urban Education* in which I coined and discussed two role identities for Black principals: the bureaucrat/administrator role identity and the ethno-humanist role identity (Lomotey, 1993). This was at a time when very little had been written about Black principals. The bureaucrat/administrator role identity, I argued, focuses on perpetuating the stratification and credentialing functions of schooling—maintaining the status quo. Of course, my definition of the ethno-humanist role identity encompassed: (1) commitment to the education of all children; (2) confidence that all children can succeed; and (3) compassion for all students, their families, and their communities. In the article, I describe a study that I undertook wherein I looked at the extent to which Black principals in a northeastern school district displayed the ethno-humanist role identity with academically successful Black students (Lomotey, 1993). That article is reprinted as Chapter 3.

## Part II

When I first wrote about Black principals in the 1980s, there were no studies that had been published specifically on Black female principals. Since that time, quite a bit has been written in journals and as dissertations about these school leaders (Bloom & Erlandson, 2003; Reed, 2012; Jean-Marie, 2013). In Chapter 4, I offer a reprint of my 2019 article (Lomotey, 2019), "Research on the Leadership of Black Women Principals: Implications for Black Students." In this article, I review studies of Black women principals. This is an important article; I uncovered no reviews of research on Black women principals prior to its publication.

In the early 1990s, literature began to appear focusing specifically on Black male principals. In Chapter 5, I offer a new investigation and summary of the research on the leadership of Black male principals (e.g., Khalifa, 2008; Henderson, 2015; Brooks, 2017).

## Part III

In Chapter 6, I extend the discussion of the ethno-humanist role identity, describing in more depth the three C's—confidence, commitment, and compassion—as they are reflected in the leadership of Black principals in schools with successful Black students. I summarize what we know about Black principals and ethno-humanism as a result of the relevant research that appeared between 1985 and 2020. I provide further clarification of the ethno-humanist role identity, citing illustrations in more recent literature, of its use, most notably, in the research of others who have borrowed the ethno-humanism terminology. (I was in university administration for 15 years. During this time, I stayed on top of the field by reading hundreds of articles a year—on urban education. I was compelled to do this as the editor of the journal *Urban Education* for 19 years. During this period, I also read extensively on the principalship and Black principals in particular.) Over the years, several scholars have built upon the ethno-humanist role identity as I had defined it (e.g., Tillman, 2004; Gooden, 2005; Henderson, 2015).

As I looked at the writings of the 1990s and beyond, I noted that the concept of CRP/T had gained substantial prominence (Ladson-Billings, 1995; Gay, 2010). I look at this work in Chapter 7. More recently, a body of work has developed focusing on CRSL (McCray & Beachum, 2011; Beachum, 2011; Gallien, 2012, Khalifa et al., 2016). In Chapter 8, I consider the notion of CRSL, a concept

# INTRODUCTION                                                    xxv

that encompasses my concept of ethno-humanism. I describe CRSL and discuss how it builds on ethno-humanism. I link it with CRP/T and to ethno-humanism.

In Chapter 9, I summarize what we know about Black principals, including a discussion of the few studies on Black principals that preceded my work. I offer a response to the query: What does it all mean for Black student success going forward? I describe the significance of this work: (1) for Black students; (2) for Black people, in general; (3) for the principalship; and (4) for U.S. education, particularly given the significant opportunity gap that continues to exist for Black children.

While education is not, as some have suggested, a cure-all, it does increase one's overall life chances. We live in a credential-oriented society; people care *whether* you've gone to school, and they care *where* you've gone to school. That may not be ideal in my mind or in the mind of the reader, but that's the way it is. Relatedly, a better understanding of the role of culture in education—and of the significance of the ethno-humanist role identity and CRSL—might help us to improve the education of Black students and increase their success. Indeed, this understanding might help us to increase the success of all students.

I expect that this book will have a wide readership. I say this because (1) very few books have been written on Black principals, (2) much of the current work on Black principals cites my earlier work, and (3) I am considered by many to be one of the pioneers in this area. Over the past 40 years, writings on Black principals have appeared primarily in doctoral dissertations, journal articles, and book chapters. Those few writings that have appeared in books have dealt with limited aspects of principal leadership. In this book, I look at several aspects of Black principal leadership in relation to ethno-humanism, CRP/T, and CRSL.

I did some of the earliest work on Black principals (Lomotey, 1985, 1987, 1989), and that work has been cited consistently through the years; my work is considered by many to be a significant part of the genesis of research on Black principals. About this, Karen Seashore (2020) said,

> It is not an overstatement to say that he [Kofi Lomotey] is the intellectual grandfather of all of our younger colleagues whose work focuses on social justice as a leadership priority. His first article—published the year before my first participation in the annual UCEA [University Council for Educational Administration] conference and later incorporated into a book—was based on a study of African American principals and was (to my knowledge) the first to explore the tensions between a focus on social justice (which he termed ethno-humanism) and the managerial aspects. (p. 1)

Here, Seashore is citing the distinction that I make between the characteristics of the bureaucrat/administrator role identity and the ethno-humanist role identity.

Scheurich (2020) added:

> Back then, he [Lomotey] was largely a solo voice, standing by himself, a Black man doing research on Black students, educators, and school leaders. This, though, is what real, impressive "commitment, excellence, and leadership" look like: standing alone, speaking and doing research that was rejected by almost everyone around him. . . . He kept coming, kept speaking, kept doing the research, kept modeling what was to come in the future, though at the time he did not know this. He did not know the arc of history would bend his way to social justice. He stood, spoke, and did because he knew how critically important to school leadership it was, that race and racism needed to be addressed. (p. 1)

With these observations in mind, a contribution from me at this time is long overdue and will, I hope, be enthusiastically welcomed within the field.

This book will, I suspect, be of interest to practicing principals and faculty who teach courses on (Black) education, school leadership, (leadership for) social justice, multicultural education, and more. The book will also, I trust, be of interest to faculty conducting research on (Black) principal leadership. For undergraduate and graduate classes, I have included discussion questions at the conclusion of each chapter—including the chapters in which I have reprinted previously published articles.

Enjoy.

# *References*

Beachum, F. (2011). Culturally relevant leadership for complex 21st-century school contexts. In F. W. Fenwick (Ed.), *The SAGE handbook of educational leadership* (pp. 26–34). SAGE.

Bloom, C. M., & Erlandson, D. A. (2003). African American women principals in urban schools: Realities, (re)constructions, and resolutions. *Educational Administration Quarterly, 39*(3), 339–369.

Bowles, S., & Gintis, H. (1976). *Schooling in capitalist America: Educational reform and the contradictions of economic life.* Basic Books.

Brooks, A. E. (2017). *A study of lived experiences of African American male principals in urban elementary schools* [Unpublished doctoral dissertation]. Bellarmine University, Louisville, KY.

Coleman, J., Campbell, E. Q., Hobson, C. J., McPartland, J., Mood, A. M., Weinfeld, F. D., & York, R. L. (1965). *Equality of educational opportunity.* U.S. Printing Office.

Gallien, E. (2012). *Culturally relevant leadership: Principal practices that support the achievement of African American males* [Unpublished doctoral dissertation]. University of Wisconsin-Madison.

Gay, G. (2010). *Culturally responsive teaching* (2nd ed.). Teachers College Press.

Gooden, M. (2005). The role of an African American principal in an urban information technology high school. *Educational Administration Quarterly, 41*(4), 630–650.

Hale-Benson, J. (1986). *Black children: Their roots, culture, and learning styles.* Johns Hopkins University Press.

Henderson, G. (2015). Leadership experiences of African American male secondary urban principals: The impact of beliefs, values, and experiences on school leadership practices. *Journal of African American Males in Education, 6*(2), 38–54.

Jean-Marie, G. (2013). The subtlety of age, gender, and race barriers: A case study of early career African American female principals. *Journal of School Leadership, 23*(3), 615–639.

Jencks, C., Smith, M., Acland, H., Bane, M. J., Cohen, D., Gintis, H., Heyns, B., & Michaelson, S. (1972). *Inequality: A reassessment of the effect of family and schooling in America.* Basic Books.

Jensen, A. (1969). How much can we boost IQ and scholastic achievement? *Harvard Educational Review, 39*(1), 1–123.

Khalifa, M. A. (2008). *Give me the worst of them, and I'll make them the best: An ethnographic study of a successful alternative school for at-risk African American children* [Unpublished doctoral dissertation]. Michigan State University, East Lansing, MI.

Khalifa, M. A., Gooden, M. A., & Davis, J. E. (2016). Culturally responsive school leadership: A synthesis of the literature. *Review of Educational Research, 86*(4), 1272–1311.

Ladson-Billings, G. (2013). Lack of achievement or loss of opportunity? In P. L. Carter & K. G. Elner (Eds.), *Closing the opportunity gap.* Oxford University Press.

Lomotey, K. (1985). *Black principals in Black elementary schools: School leadership and school success* [Unpublished doctoral dissertation]. Stanford University, Stanford, CA.

Lomotey, K. (1987). Black principals for Black students: Some preliminary observations. *Urban Education, 22*(2), 173–181.

Lomotey, K. (1989). Cultural diversity in the urban school: Implications for principals. *NASSP Bulletin, 73*(521), 81–85.

Lomotey, K. (1990). Qualities shared by African-American principals in effective schools: A preliminary analysis. In K. Lomotey (Ed.), *Going to school: The African-American experience* (pp. 181–195). SUNY Press.

Lomotey, K. (1993). African American principals: Bureaucrat/administrators and ethno-humanists. *Urban Education, 27*(4), 395–412.

Lomotey, K. (2019). Research on the leadership of Black women principals: Implications for Black students. *Educational Researcher, 48*(6), 336–348.

Lomotey, K., & Aboh, S. (2009). Historically Black colleges and universities: Catalysts to liberation? In L. C. Tillman (Ed.), *The SAGE handbook of African American education* (pp. 311–318). SAGE.

McCray, C., & Beachum, F. (2011). Culturally relevant leadership for the enhancement of teaching and learning in urban schools. In T. Townsend & J. MacBeth (Eds.), *The international handbook of leadership for learning* (pp. 487–502). Springer.

Nobles, W. W. (1978). *African consciousness and liberation struggles: Implications for the development and construction of scientific paradigms* (Unpublished paper).

Ogbu, J. (1978). *Minority education and caste: The American system in cross-cultural perspective.* Academic.

Reed, L. C. (2012). The intersection of race and gender in school leadership for three Black female principals. *International Journal of Qualitative Studies in Education, 25*(1), 39–58.

Scheurich, J. (2020, May 24). *Letter to the UCEA Campbell Award Committee.* Copy in possession of Kofi Lomotey.

Seashore, K. (2020, June 25). *Letter to the UCEA Campbell Award Committee.* Copy in possession of Kofi Lomotey.

Shockley, W. (1972). A debate challenge: Geneticity is 80% for white identical twins' IQ's. *Phi Delta Kappan, 53*(6), 415–419.

Shujaa, M. J. (1993). Education and schooling: You can have one without the other. *Urban Education, 27*(4), 328–351.

Spring, J. (1991). Knowledge and power in research into the politics of urban education. In J. G. Cibulka, R. J. Reed, & K. K. Wong (Eds.), *The politics of urban education in the United States* (pp. 45–56). Taylor and Francis.

Tillman, L. (2004). African American principals and the legacy of Brown. *Review of Research in Education, 28*(1), 101–146.

Van Sertima, I. (1976). *They came before Columbus: The African presence in ancient America.* Random House.

Wilson, A. (1987). *The developmental psychology of the Black child.* Africana Research.

# PART ONE:
## My Early Work

# 1.

# MY BEGINNINGS: NEW YORK CITY, OBERLIN, AND STANFORD

I was born in Harlem, then a predominantly Black community in Manhattan, one of the five boroughs of New York City. When I was about six months old, my parents and my maternal grandfather (who resided with us) felt it would be "safer" to live in Queens, another borough of New York City—and so we moved to Jamaica, Queens. The new neighborhood was also largely Black. My elder sister and my only sibling, Saundra Kelley, and I attended Public School 123, a predominantly Black elementary school where we generally felt *equal to* others. In this chapter, my allusions to "equal to," "better than," and "less than" refer to how I felt when I compared myself to my peers, who, once I moved to junior high school, were mostly White. That is, I am referring generally to my level of self-confidence, and, specifically, to my confidence in my ability to succeed academically. These references speak to the level of self-assurance, or lack thereof, I displayed in interactions, in my academic work, and in virtually all levels of interactions with my peers.

From a very early age, I knew that my mother wanted me to do well in life, believed that I could do well, and consistently provided a quiet, yet nurturing, environment. The same motivation was evident from my sister; lovingly, she pushed me academically from very early on.

Saundra and I could walk to 123. She did well there academically, and I did okay. Problematically, I had a big mouth, something that people who know me today find surprising. For example, when I was in the fifth grade, my teacher said that railroad tracks meet down the road. Of course, that is not true (though I think I understood the point she was trying to make). I immediately said, "That's a lie!" I was sent to the principal's office and my mother had to come to school to meet with the principal.

My sister is two years older than I and she used to protect me—all the time. Part of the reason that I needed protection was because I had a strange misconception regarding the significance of age; I believed that if someone was older than me, they could beat me in a fight—and everyone else on our street was older than me. So, whenever I got in a fight, I basically stood there and let the opponent whip me—until my sister came. I do not mention this because I am proud of it; I mention it because it played a role in where I attended junior high school (JHS).

I feel compelled to mention that these massacres did eventually come to an end. When I was about 12 or 13, George Watson sent a *wolf ticket* to me from around the corner where he lived. (A wolf ticket is an empty threat, promise or bluff.) Everyone on my block heard it and I was compelled to respond. I went around the corner—with everyone from my block following—and I went to his house, called him out, and, when he came out, I commenced beating him mercilessly. I beat him so badly that his mother came out and told him that, if he didn't fight back, his father was going to whip him when he returned home from work; he didn't fight back. I don't recall having any other fights after that.

My father and grandfather had both transitioned by the time we went to JHS. My father committed suicide when I was six; I don't remember him very well. My grandfather succumbed to complications from lung cancer when I was 11; I remember him better. My grandfather—a retired cigar maker, who was born and raised in Kingston, Jamaica—was, no doubt, one of my first mentors. Though he—like both of my parents—had not gone past high school, he pushed me academically, displaying unending confidence in my abilities.

Shimer was our neighborhood JHS—a seventh- through ninth-grade school; we could walk there too. It was a pretty rough school, which is another way of saying it was dangerous. My mother had

MY BEGINNINGS                                                                3

a great plan. Saundra and I could both go to Shimer because she
assumed that when I got there and went to the seventh grade, my
sister would still be there—in the ninth grade—to protect me.
Unfortunately—for my mother's plan—when my sister went to
Shimer, she continued to do well academically and was quickly
skipped from the seventh to the eighth grade—which meant that
she would not be there when I arrived!

My mother switched gears and devised a new plan; she made
arrangements for me to go to JHS 125 in Woodside. I had to take
a bus and two trains to complete the 90-minute trip to 125! JHS
125 was a predominantly White school in a largely White neighborhood, and this was a totally new experience for me. I had never
been around so many White people—peers or adults.

I felt *less than* in 125, in that the student, teacher, and administrator differences and the prevailing cultural norms made me less
confident that I could achieve anything that I desired. I also noted
the disparities in human and material resources. However, I did
well enough to pass the test to get into Brooklyn Technical High
School (Tech). Tech—at that time an all-boys school—is still one
of the top three public high schools in New York City, along with
Bronx High School of Science and Peter Stuyvesant High School.
I entered Tech in the ninth grade. I survived at Tech because I did
very well in math, and I was on the basketball team. Still, despite
my math skills and being on the basketball team, I felt *less than*
at Tech.

At the end of my junior year at Tech, I transferred to Springfield Gardens High School—my neighborhood high school—and
graduated from Springfield Gardens the next year.

In part, as a function of feeling *less than*, I did not intend to go
to college when I graduated from high school. Instead, I got married to Yolanda Jenkins, we had a daughter, Shawnjua Tien Kelley
(aka Faida), and, for two years, I worked on Wall Street during the
day and drove a yellow cab at night. Many of the guys with whom I
hung out during this time were not positive influences for me. With
no stretch of the imagination could they be considered mentors.

Through this period, my experiences were not particularly positive, and these were, perhaps, the darkest years of my life.

After two years, I noticed that there were few people on Wall Street who looked like me, who were making more money than I; the writing was on the wall (or on the ceiling)—a glass ceiling. Luckily for me, Saundra was close friends with a guy who was a student at Oberlin College, Michael Lythcott; Michael knew someone who worked in the admissions office. She told him she had a brother who needed to go to college. The admissions officer arranged for an off-campus interview, and the rest is history—as I began a new pathway to my future. I went to Oberlin, where I played basketball. I definitely felt *less than* at Oberlin, a small, elite, predominantly White, liberal arts college. My feelings of being *less than* at Oberlin meant that, although I excelled in math, which partly led to my admission to the College, I lasted only a year in that major.

I chose math initially because I did well in math in high school. But having been out of school for two years, working on Wall Street, I should have started with pre-calculus at Oberlin; instead, I went right into calculus. Notably, there were only two other Black students in my calculus class—and they were both repeating calculus! I "successfully" completed a year of calculus, but I didn't enjoy it. In my second year, I switched my major to economics. (I was under the illusion that economics is related to mathematics.)

I had five very significant mentors at Oberlin: Omowale Babalawo (aka Frank Satterwhite), Yakubu Saaka, Booker Peek, Hal D. Payne, and Aama Nahuja. A while after I arrived at Oberlin, my first wife, Yolanda, and I separated, and we divorced shortly thereafter. Nahuja and I would marry in 1977.

At Oberlin, I became interested in education. That interest was sparked because of my interactions with these people, perhaps most notably Booker Peek, an Oberlin faculty member. Booker joined the Oberlin faculty in 1970, the year I arrived there as a freshperson. He had an unusual faculty contract, as I recall. He was not expected to publish; the College's expectation for Booker

MY BEGINNINGS

was that, in addition to teaching, he was to strengthen the relationship between the College and the local K–12 schools. That he
did. Though a relatively small town with slightly more than 10,000
people, Oberlin had a Black population of about 6,000 (60%).

As it was/is throughout this country (as I had begun to learn),
Black students did not perform as well as their White counterparts
in the Oberlin schools; the contrast was devastating. Booker was
constantly engaged with the schools, attempting to address the
disenfranchisement of Black children. He regularly had tutorial
programs operating—often in his home—with College students,
including me, providing the tutoring. When Black students were
suspended from Oberlin High School, Booker arranged for them
to be "released to him." He would have them tutored in his home
by his family members and by students at the College. Ten years
after leaving Oberlin, I edited a book on Black education (Lomotey,
1990). I interviewed Booker and included the interview in the book.
In my editor's note preceding the transcript of the interview, I wrote
(Lomotey, 1990), in part, the following:

> [Peek] has been deeply committed to the education of all
> students—particularly African-American students—from
> preschool to professional school. He is personally respon-
> sible for the academic success of literally hundreds of
> students in Oberlin's public schools, its College, and in
> several undergraduate, graduate, and professional schools
> across the country. Year round, Peek runs tutorial pro-
> grams for students of all ages—often in his own home or
> office and usually with his own funds. . .
>
> By his genius and his practice, Peek has created an environ-
> ment worthy of scholarly treatment. I pleaded with him to
> write for this volume; he respectfully declined. Still, I felt
> that it was important that what he had to say be shared
> with an audience larger than Oberlin. . . . What follows is
> the alternative: an interview. It is a tribute to a man who,

in my mind, best exemplifies a lifelong commitment to the education of African-American people. (p. 12)

Booker is indeed a mentor for me; he cared about my academic success, pushed me to excel, and clearly—to this day—displays compassion for me and for others in our community.

My commitment to Black people was also enhanced tremendously because of my interaction with Omowale Babalawo and Yakubu Saaka. Omowale was an administrator at Oberlin who had earned his PhD at Stanford. He is a pan-African nationalist. While at Oberlin, I served as his student assistant. A significant part of my responsibility in that capacity was to liaise between him and the various social activist organizations in which he was involved. One such organization was the Council of Independent Black Institutions (CIBI). CIBI is an umbrella organization for independent African-centered schools. Omowale helped found the organization in 1972. The experience of working with Omowale introduced me to independent African-centered schools and added a new dimension to my understanding of the education of Black children.

Omowale continues to inspire me, though I do not see him or talk with him often. He was committed to my education—not just at Oberlin and not just "in the classroom," but in my broader worldliness and in my schooling beyond the undergraduate experience. In addition to (1) hiring me as a student assistant—when technically he had no student positions available, (2) introducing me to the various progressive organizations of which he was a part, and (3) inspiring me to go on to graduate school, Omowale helped me to become engaged in other aspects of the College. For example, he appointed me as a member of the committee that developed the African American Community and Student Development Program (AACSDP)—Oberlin's Black Studies program, as it was called at that time. He clearly displayed compassion for me and for the Black community.

In the summer following my junior year at Oberlin (1973), I traveled with a group of Oberlin students to Ghana and Nigeria in West

MY BEGINNINGS

Africa. Omowale led the group. While in Ghana, I befriended a graduate student at the University of Ghana: Yakubu Saaka. As I recall, Omowale arranged for Yakubu to return to Oberlin with us. Yakubu served as a professor at Oberlin while enrolled in the doctoral program in political science at Case Western Reserve University in Cleveland, Ohio. Yakubu and I became very close friends; in fact, we shared an apartment in Oberlin for a few years. In 1977, we traveled together with a group of Black educators to the People's Republic of China. I learned quite a bit about the world, Africa, and Ghana specifically as a result of my relationship with Yakubu, who made his final transition in 2008. In addition to being committed to his own education, Yakubu displayed a commitment to my education. Along with Omowale, he encouraged me to go to graduate school at Stanford.

Hal Payne was another person who inspired me at Oberlin. Hal was the Dean of Developmental Services; he was Oberlin's "Black Dean" in the early 1970s. Part of Hal's responsibility was chairing the College's Academic Standing Committee. This was the committee that, each year, determined what would happen to students who had not done well academically during the preceding academic year. (Nearly every college has such a committee.) I was asked to serve on the Committee as the student representative in my sophomore year and served for three years. I recall that the case of one particular Black STEM major was brought before the Committee every year that I served. Each year I pleaded with Committee members to not dismiss him. Each year they agreed. He ended up graduating from Oberlin with a STEM degree and went on to earn a PhD at MIT. (I think he was the first Black male student to graduate from Oberlin with a degree in his field.) Most importantly, serving on that Committee helped me to understand much of the intricate workings of the College. To this day, I am appreciative of the confidence that Hal placed in me by appointing me to that Committee.

In my junior year at Oberlin, I told Omowale that I wanted to start an independent African-centered school for Black children. He sat back in his seat and, in a matter-of-fact fashion, said, "Well, do it." He went on to suggest that I spend some time with Kasisi Jitu Weusi, the founding director of Uhuru Sasa Shule, an independent African-centered school in Brooklyn, New York. Jitu was the Executive Director of CIBI. He had been one of the founding members, with Omowale and several others.

A few months later, I traveled to Brooklyn and spent several days—and nights—at Uhuru Sasa Shule at the feet of Jitu. I learned quite a bit from that experience and grew close to Jitu as a result of that opportunity. In fact, when he stepped down as head of CIBI in 1976, I was selected to replace him and served in that capacity for 11 years. (Currently, I am the Secretary/Treasurer of CIBI, a position that I have held since 1987.) Jitu made his final transition in 2013.

I have never been optimistic about the potential for the success of Black students in U.S. public schools; these institutions have *never* worked for the benefit of the majority of Black children. So, after visiting Uhuru Sasa Shule, I started and became the administrator of an African-centered preschool in February 1973. In deciding how to spend my 24 hours each day, I quit the basketball team—and almost everything else except *required* schoolwork.

In seeking to recruit preschoolers for the school, I asked Booker and Hal if I could enroll their 4-year-old daughters, who were both named Angela. They both agreed. I then went door-to-door in the community surrounding the College and recruited two more Black 4-year-olds. We started in a room in Afrikan Heritage House—the Black student residence hall—on the Oberlin campus. The Director, Ura Jones, did not use her office much and agreed to allow us to convert it to a classroom. Oberlin students taught in the Shule. In May of that year, we moved the Shule to a three-bedroom apartment and increased our enrollment to 17. In Fall of 1973, we moved into Carter's Nursing Home, a Black-owned senior residence. Their second floor was vacant, and we rented several rooms there. At maximum, our enrolment increased to about 35 children aged 4 to 8 years.

I started the African-centered preschool, Shule ya Kujitambua— The School for Black Re-Identification, in Kiswahili—as I was

MY BEGINNINGS                                          9

beginning to better understand that the experiences of Black children and White children in school were/are substantially different (Lomotey, 1990). I was convinced that if we were to provide a culturally responsive pedagogy/teaching experience for Black children, they, too, would do well academically (Shockley & Lomotey, 2020). When I speak of a culturally responsive pedagogy/teaching experience, among other things, I am referring to: (1) children "seeing themselves in the curriculum," (2) children seeing "successful" people who look like them, (3) educators teaching with illustrations that children can relate to in their environment, and (4) children seeing at least some teachers who look like them (Eubanks & Weaver, 1999; Lomotey, 1989).

This thinking on my part was largely because of my interactions with Omowale, Booker, and Yakubu and the myriad experiences in which they encouraged me to participate. One thing that my interactions with these heroes did for me was to encourage me to read. My academic performance at Oberlin was "nothing to write home about." However, I did spend quite a bit of time at Oberlin reading about Black people. This was quite significant because I did not like reading—at all—while in elementary, junior high, and high school. Some of these newfound reading opportunities arose in classes, and others arose outside of class. For example, I, along with several other Black students, had a study group associated with the All-African People's Revolutionary Party (AAPRP) wherein we regularly read the works of Kwame Nkrumah and other African and African American leaders. Even though I majored in economics, earning 24 credit hours in that area, I earned more than 40 credit hours in Black Studies, taking courses with Booker, Omowale, Yakubu, and several other Black Studies scholars.

Another interesting educational experience that I had while at Oberlin was establishing what was called the Friday Night Lecture Series in 1973. I came up with the idea and went to the Afrikan Heritage House Director, Ura Jones; the Black Student Association (Abusua) President, Mark Holbert; the Black Studies Director, Omowale; and Dean Hal Payne, and asked them each for funds to start the Series. All in all, I collected $7,500 in that first year—which was quite significant back then. We brought in "everyone who was anyone" in the next several years, including Yosef ben Jochannon, Sonia Sanchez, John Henrik Clarke, Nikki Giovanni, Ivan Van Sertima, Naim Akbar, Kathleen Cleaver, Louis Farrakhan, Jessie Jackson, Haki Madhubuti, Maulana Karenga, and many more.

For me, the most powerful thing about this experience was that I did almost everything associated with the Series by myself. I contacted the speakers (or their agents). I picked them up at the Cleveland Airport and drove them to Oberlin. I introduced them when they lectured. I sat with them at dinner. I transported them to and from their hotel room. And I transported them back to the airport. This provided a tremendous and unique opportunity for me to talk with and learn from these superstars. In their own way, many of them demonstrated commitment to me, confidence in my abilities, and compassion for me and for our community.

I was accepted into Stanford's doctoral program in educational leadership—straight out of undergraduate school. Once I got over the excitement, I went back to what I was doing, because I was in the middle of operating the Shule and because I could not imagine having enough money to go to graduate school at Stanford—or anywhere else. (I vividly remember Yakubu saying to me with his West African accent, "What are you talking about? Nobody pays to get a doctoral degree!") I had applied to Stanford, in part, because Omowale had earned his PhD in educational leadership at Stanford. After declining my acceptance into Stanford's PhD program, I continued working with the preschool for three more years and then reapplied to Stanford. To my pleasure and surprise, they admitted me again! By this time, Yolanda and I had divorced and I had married Nahuja, my current wife of 45 years. (I think this one is going to last!) This time I decided to accept the invitation to seek a PhD in the Stanford University School of Education.

I met Nahuja when she applied to teach at the preschool that I had started on the Oberlin campus. She was a sophomore whose family lived in Germany; her father was an engineer for the

MY BEGINNINGS                                                        11

U.S. government and they always resided near Air Force bases—he designed barracks and hangers. We started dating shortly thereafter and married four years later in 1977. I include her as one of my mentors at Oberlin for very different reasons. It wasn't necessarily anything that she said or even that she did. (I remember telling Nahuja's sister, chaille maddox, who was also enrolled at Oberlin at the time, that I found Nahuja "appealing.") Being with Nahuja while also being involved in the preschool inspired me to do several things. I stopped smoking. (I had been smoking 2.5 packs of cigarettes a day!) I started reading more and working harder academically. I stopped womanizing and using illicit drugs. I became more serious about my academic life. I would discuss my papers with Nahuja, and she would read drafts of what I would write and provide useful feedback. When we left Oberlin, in 1979, with our first son, Juba, in tow, I thought I was ready for Stanford; I was not.

While preparing to go to Stanford, I got a letter indicating that a woman by the name of Barbara Hatton was going to be my faculty advisor. I was excited when I learned that Dr. Hatton was Black. However, when I got there and went to see her in her office, she was packing her books; she was leaving Stanford! At the time, she was the only full-time Black faculty member in the entire Stanford School of Education! This was indeed discouraging.

Fortunately, I soon met others while at Stanford, including Gloria Ladson-Billings, who was also a doctoral student at Stanford at that time and Joyce King, another African American woman, who had earned her PhD from Stanford and was an adjunct professor in the Stanford School of Education. Joyce became a friend, a mentor, and a colleague and remains so after more than 40 years. Joyce is now the Benjamin E. Mays Endowed Chair for Urban Teaching and Professor of Educational Policy Studies in the College of Education and Human Development at Georgia State University in Atlanta.

Throughout my classwork at Stanford and into the first year writing the dissertation, I again felt *less than*. Despite that feeling, I was highly motivated to earn the Stanford PhD This was true, in part, because I had connected getting the degree with being able to play a more significant role in the education of Black children. Every day after class I would hurry to East Palo Alto, a nearby Black community, to work with Shule Ya Taifa (The School for the Nation), another African-centered school that I co-founded; I was getting this degree to help Black children—and Black people.

I was also motivated by the fact that, at that time, Stanford's School of Education was rated number one in the country. I had already begun to understand that we live in a credential-oriented society; people care if you've gone to school—and they care *where* you've gone to school. That, of course, is not ideal in my mind—and perhaps in the reader's mind—but it is the way the world operates.

Then something inspired me to start reading more—and speed reading—and to substantially improve my writing. Three Stanford professors provided much of the motivation: Larry Cuban, Milbrey McLaughlin, and the late Ed Bridges. My motivation stemmed from their helping me to identify and explain ideas and methodologies that inspired me to complete my course of study and to carve out a meaningful research agenda intended to address the education of Black people. They taught me that good writing and intelligence are not measured by the length of your words and sentences, but, instead, by the extent to which people can understand what you write. They believed in me and in my potential—before I did. From that point to this one, I ceased feeling *less than*. I feel *equal to*—and in some cases (much) *better than*!

These experiences in New York, Oberlin, and Stanford are important because they helped me to develop my interest in leadership and my leadership skills. Operating the Lecture Series was an opportunity to lead. Serving on the Academic Standing Committee was an opportunity in leadership. Starting and operating Shule ya Kujitambua in Oberlin and Shule ya Taifa in California were important leadership opportunities.

These experiences were also significant because of the people who influenced me and taught me the importance of having confidence in, commitment to, and compassion for people. I believe that—in large part, because of these experiences—as a teacher I display more confidence in my students, increased commitment to their success, and added compassion for them. Perhaps most importantly, I have learned that these qualities are important for teachers *and* leaders.

## *Discussion Questions*

1. Discuss instances, while growing up, where you felt "less than," "equal to," or "better than" your peers or others who were around you.

2. Describe your mentors while you were growing up and through the years.

## *References*

Eubanks, S. C., & Weaver, R. (1999). Excellence through diversity: Connecting the teacher quality and teacher diversity agendas. *The Journal of Negro Education, 68*(3), 451–459.

Lomotey, K. (1989). Cultural diversity in the urban school: Implications for principals. *NASSP Bulletin, 73*(521), 81–85.

Lomotey, K. (Ed.). (1990). *Going to school: The African-American experience.* State University of New York Press.

Shockley, K. G., & Lomotey, K. (Eds.). (2020). *African-centered education: Theory and practice.* Myers Education Press.

# 2.

# BLACK PRINCIPALS FOR BLACK STUDENTS:
## SOME PRELIMINARY OBSERVATIONS[1]

*When I enrolled at Stanford to pursue my PhD in educational leadership, I was clearly interested in Black education, but I didn't know exactly what I wanted to explore in my dissertation. I had been thinking about the nature of social science research in general and education research in particular; at that time (1979) the large majority of social science research was conducted with White male samples, and there was usually an unspoken assumption that the findings derived from those studies applied to White women and to Black, Latinx, and Indigenous Peoples.*

*I had been doing quite a bit of reading during that period on so-called effective schools: the work of Edmonds (1979), Brookover et al. (1978), Frederiksen (1975), and others. I began to wonder if, in fact, the qualities identified for principals in effective schools—qualities derived from studies of White male principals in effective schools—were characteristics that Black principals in effective schools possessed. That is, the literature said that successful principals stress goal development, energy harnessing, communication facilitation, and instructional leadership. I wondered, if one were to study successful Black principals, would they observe the same qualities?*

*With a sample of three successful Black elementary school principals, I went about the business of exploring this question in my dissertation*

---

1. REPRINT Lomotey, K. (1987). Black principals for Black students: Some preliminary observations. *Urban Education, 22*(2), 173–181.

*and in subsequent research. In the final analysis, I discovered that these principals did indeed display the characteristics noted in the literature for principals in effective schools: goal development, energy harnessing, communication facilitation, and instructional leadership.*

*I also wondered if successful Black principals held any qualities in common with each other, aside from the qualities that the literature said that more successful principals possessed. In my dissertation research, I also noted other characteristics that they held in common with each other: confidence in the abilities of all their students to do well academically, commitment to the education of all their students, and compassion for all their students, their families, and their communities. If Brookover and Lezotte (1979) and Rist (1973) are right, these characteristics are important. These researchers suggested that principals influence teachers who, in turn, influence students. Principals displaying confidence, commitment, and compassion is indeed critical if, in fact, principals are going to positively influence the attitudes and behavior of teachers. That is, if there is a desire for teachers to be confident, committed, and compassionate, principals should possess these characteristics and stress them in professional development activities and in other regular interactions with teachers, students, parents, and other community members. This is a point to which I return later in this book. The study reprinted in this chapter describes in detail my findings related to these two questions.*

*Enjoy!*

*Cultural differences seem to make black principals more effective in black schools.*

# BLACK PRINCIPALS FOR BLACK STUDENTS
## Some Preliminary Observations

*KOFI LOMOTEY*
*SUNY-Buffalo*

I recently concluded an exploratory study that looks at the impact of the leadership of black principals (in predominantly black elementary schools) on the academic achievement of their students. In this article, I use the results of my study, coupled with the limited additional evidence, to speculate that (1) black principals positively affect the academic achievement of black students and (2) black leaders-and black principals, in particular—lead differently than their white peers. I further speculate that a separate body of research on the relationship between black principal leadership and black student achievement could yield results that differ from those that have been obtained thus far in the general research. I discuss these two bodies of evidence separately, coupled with evidence from my own exploratory study.

First, culture is important when looking at the significance of the black principals' influence upon black students. Blacks have a distinct culture in America. This view has been disputed in the literature, but is generally accepted now (Blauner, 1972; Pinkney, 1976).[1] Culture can be defined by offering its seven components-mythology, ethos, creative motif, political organization, economic organization, social organization, and history (Karenga, 1980). Each ethnic group has these seven characteristics, and it is the uniqueness of the makeup of each quality and of the combination of these seven qualities in a given ethnic group that determine the way a group, and the individuals within it, relates to the world.

There is, however, another body of literature that suggests that race is becoming less important while class is becoming more important in the behavior of blacks and other ethnic groups (Wilson, 1980;

Sowell, 1981).[2] While I acknowledge the impact of socioeconomic status on behavior, I contend that the culture of a people defines (1) situations; (2) attitudes, values, and goals; (3) myths, legends, and the supernatural; and (4) behavior patterns (Horton and Hunt, 1964).

The way that a person relates to others and to circumstances that they encounter is shaped by the culture of that individual. Within this perspective, black people respond differently to situations than do people from other cultures in America. Consider, for example, a black principal about to discipline a black student. If we assume that race culture is more significant than class culture, the principal would, consciously or unconsciously, draw upon black cultural views with regard to discipline (i.e., the ways that blacks, as a race, have historically looked upon and dealt with discipline). He or she would also consider the situation, understanding it in a way that a non-black might not be able, given the different cultural basis of looking at the world. It is then that they would respond to the situation, having gone through a thought process made possible by their unique cultural characteristics.

A black principal whom I interviewed explains:

> In this school environment parents believe in corporal punishment, but I had new teachers who don't come from this culture [ and] who did not believe in corporal punishment. No one uses corporal punishment here but me, when it's used. You have to look at those values that the people hold dear and build on those. You can't just look at what society's asking as a whole and say I'm gonna run my school according to what is happening now. A good example being individualization of instruction, the learning center approach and all the kinds of things that came out several years ago. That would not work in a black school because the children could not handle the freedom of scheduling and whatever. You'd have to start with a very structured background with the youngsters and then build into teaching children how to schedule because that was just too much.

So you have to look at, again, the culture, the values, those kinds of objectives you want articulated for your children. And then you have to be the one to see that they're implemented, whether it be monitoring those teachers [or] selecting those teachers. (Lomotey, 1985, p. 169)

The principal's comments illustrate the value of black principals working with black students.

On the other hand, Sowell and others might argue that such a principal would be influenced primarily by his or her socioeconomic status, say middle class, and respond accordingly to a, say, lower-class, child.

Looking at the relationship between black principals and black students from another perspective, it has been acknowledged that effective communication or interaction comes about when two people are similar (MacLennan, 1975). This concept is known as homophily (Rogers and Shoemaker, 1971). People who have homogeneous beliefs, values, attributes, education, or social status tend to interact and communicate more effectively with each other (Kochman, 1981). When two blacks interact or communicate, their shared beliefs and values suggest that homophily occurs, bringing about greater information usage, attitude formation, attitude change, and behavior change. For example, homophily occurs in the communication and interaction between a black principal and black students, as a result of their likenesses. This may be a desirable situation because this homophily may make interaction and the exchange of thoughts and messages more effective and beneficial to all involved, ultimately affecting academic achievement. The black principal quoted earlier discussed her relationship with her students in a way that reflected this kinship embodied in homophily:

When I say poor background, it's generally an unorganized home background. Mother going one way, whether it's going to work or family going one way. The family structure isn't very close. There's no father in the home. So, it looks as if, as I look at it, the black principal has to be the one almost looking and playing God sometimes, in terms of looking at values, looking at past history. . . . No matter what new innovations or methods are coming in education you have to look at the needs of your children, the cultural background of your children. . . . You have to go back and look at how we, as a people, functioned. The extended family that was once very important died out and I'm finding at a school like this we have a gang problem because we don't have extended families. We have problems of child care with kindergarteners going home at noon, or we have, for example, kindergarteners whose mothers have to work and they set a clock 'cause the kid can't tell when to go to school. The mother dresses the 5-year-old. She sets the clock. When the clock rings you push a little button and then you leave to go to school. That shouldn't be. With extended families, we didn't have that kind of problem. You didn't have children just walking the streets alone. You had brothers, sisters, uncles [and] cousins, who helped with school work and whatever. Now you have a totally different problem existing because we are saying that was something that was no good or whatever we say. So I think you first have to look at culture. That's most important. You have to look at what functions for the culture. (Lomotey, 1985, pp. 159-60)

This principal's comments reflect an understanding of her students that comes about, presumably, through homophily.

A brief look at the relationship between black teachers and black students is instructive. Research suggests that teacher race may have an impact on student achievement. A few researchers have found that black teachers can positively affect the achievement of black students (Murnane, 1975; Spady, 1973; Greenleigh Associates, 1966). In this research, the academic achievement scores of black students with black teachers and the scores of black students with white teachers were compared. The results of these studies show that scores of the black students with black teachers were higher, suggesting that black students do better academically with teachers of their own racial background. One may infer from this that black principals might also have a positive effect on the academic achievement of black students again owing to cultural similarities.[3] A rationale for this speculation is provided by the following comment made by a black principal in my study, where he discusses his attitude toward the academic potential of black students:

> I think we're doing an excellent job, but that doesn't mean that we're pleased. Because actually, our goal would be to have something like 70 to 75% of the children achieving on the CTBS and I think that is attainable. . . . But the point is that I believe that this can be attained with the present community [ and] with the present children.
>
> The basic philosophy we try to have here with the staff and with the leadership is that we're not content or satisfied with our success. If one child is not achieving at his maximum potential, or close to that maximum potential, then we've failed. (Lomotey, 1985, p. 163)

This confidence held by a black principal in his black students could be culturally linked and certainly could contribute, directly and indirectly, to the success of his students.

There is an argument that black and white leaders do lead differently. In the area of education, black principals seem to place a higher priority on community involvement in the educational milieu than do their white colleagues (Monteiro, 1977). They are more inclined, as a group, to involve parents and other community members in school activities and, to a degree, in decision making. They view such involvement as fundamental to the overall success of the school and to their individual success. Black principals may be less threatened by a focus on community relations, as they tend to relate more closely with the larger community. In black schools,[4] it is possible that this emphasis on the larger community may be a key ingredient in bringing about improved academic performance for black students. It is also possible that black principals are able to weave this relationship (in a way that would be elusive to principals of other races) because of the similarity between their attitudes, values, and goals and those of the larger black community.

In my own study, I found that the black principals in black schools shared a common quality: a deep compassion for their students and for the communities in which they (the students) lived. One black teacher, who works with a black principal, discussed the impact that this compassion has on students:

> They can relate to a black principal because the principal is a mother or father figure. . . . I think when she [Ms. Marshall] speaks . . . they're used to that authoritative woman at home too. [Marie] [Marshall] has that softness . . . where the kids are free to come up to her and hug her and, yet in still, they know she might paddle their butts the next day. So I think there's a nice balance between the kids and [Marie] where they'll work hard when she asks them to. They know they're gonna get some type of reward or they're gonna get praised or they know they're gonna be scolded or they're gonna be paddled—some of them. I think they've got that love 'cause she's like a mama. You know they're gonna get it.
>
> In school you're here to learn and plus she's a good role model. . . . They feel free to run up and touch her. A lot of times teachers don't want you to touch them. It's a nice feeling where they feel close to her and they try to achieve. (Lomotey, 1985, p. 158)

Subordinates may react differently to their supervisor depending upon the supervisor's race (Parker, 1976). If subordinates react differently to supervisors based upon the supervisor's race, this could affect the leadership of the supervisor along racial lines, again differentiating the leadership of black and white leaders. For example, a white teacher whom I interviewed suggests strongly, in the following excerpt, that her behavior (and perhaps the behavior of her peers) is severely affected by the leadership of the black principal in her school:

> I know that the child is very important [to him]. Mr. [Brooks] has spoken to us more than once on how to make our children feel good about themselves and [about the fact that] they have rights and that we are to treat them as we want to be treated. [In addition, he stresses that] bad conduct will not be tolerated. Also, self value is very, very important here and is stressed along with responsibility.
>
> I've been stifled in other areas because my administrator's priorities were not with the kids and that's frustrating. And that's why I'm feeling really at home here because this is a unique school. Everything that Mr. [Brooks] does, I really believe, is in the kids' best interest. And you can really tell because he goes to his teachers and finds out. He's just squared away in that area. It's what's best for the kids and then everything else is secondary.
>
> The first week of school, I had 43 kids and I just thought that was terrible for me. And he said, no, it's not for you I'm worried. It's the kids. He goes, you can't feel sorry for yourself. You gotta feel sorry for the kids. And it's true. It was bad on me, but it was worse for them. He just really has it together in that area, as far as I can see. (Lomotey, 1985, p. 152-53)

This teacher's behavior is certainly affected as a result of the influence of her principal's (seemingly culturally based) attitude and leadership. One would suspect that the behavior of her peers would be affected similarly.

These few school leadership studies and general leadership studies that consider the effect of race, coupled with my own research, suggest that black principals may exercise leadership differently. Similarly, the race of the principal may affect black academic achievement, and black and white principals may lead differently. It is clear that additional research, exploratory and theory-testing, will need to be done in this and related areas.

## *Notes*

1. The argument of the opponents of this view is based on the assertion that the elimination of African cultural heritage brought about a total acculturation of blacks and that their culture is, therefore, influenced solely by the American culture (Myrdal, 1944; Glazer and Moynihan, 1964; Frazier, 1964; Banfield, 1970). Herskovits, a cultural anthropologist, and others have long acknowledged a black culture, arguing that there are black ethnic patterns that are African influenced (Herskovits, 1942; Sarason, 1973; Havighurst, 1976). While my view is not that the culture of blacks in America is identical to that obtained in any part of Africa, I do hold that blacks in America have combined their African heritage with the American experience to create a unique black culture, much in the same way that other ethnic groups in America have developed their own distinguishable cultures. An appreciation for this duality in black cultures is acknowledged by many social scientists including DuBois (DuBois, 1961).

2. Scholars who support this contention argue that while race is unyieldingly important in America, a monolithic view of the black presence in America obscures the significant differences in experiences obtained by the various classes of blacks (Wilson, 1980; Sowell, 1981). In fact, as early as 1947, Davis and Havighurst conducted a study in which they interviewed black and white, lower- and middle-class mothers and concluded that class differences are more significant than color differences in the development of one's personality. While I acknowledge that all groups have class cultures as well as a race culture (Havighurst, 1976; Hale, 1982), my view, like that of Karenga and others, is that the impact of the race culture predominates (Karenga, 1978; Hale, 1982; Stodolsky and Lesser, 1967).

3.  This logic assumes that principals influence teachers, who, in turn, influence students to bring about more successful schools. This line of reasoning is supported in the effective schools literature (Brookover & Lezotte, 1979; Rist, 1973).
4.  "Black schools" are defined herein as schools that have a student population that is predominantly black.

## *References*

BANFIELD, E. (1970) The Unheavenly City. Boston: Little, Brown.

BLAUNER, R. (1972) Racial Oppression in America. New York: Harper & Row.

BROOKOVER, W. B. and L. W. LEZOTTE (1979) Changes in School Characteristics Coincident with Changes in Student Achievement. East Lansing: Michigan State University, College of Urban Development.

DuBOIS, W.E.B. (1961) The Souls of Black Folk: Essays and Sketches. New York: Fawcett.

FRAZIER, E. F. (1964) The Negro in the United States. New York: Macmillan.

GLAZER, N. and D. P. MOYNIHAN (1964) Beyond the Melting Pot: The Negroes, Puerto Ricans, Jews, Italians, and Irish of New York City. Cambridge: MIT Press.

Greenleigh Associates (1966) Field Test and Evaluation of Selected Adult Basic Education Systems. New York: Author.

HALE, J. (1982) Black Children, Their Roots, Culture, and Learning Styles. Provo, UT: Brigham Young Univ. Press.

HAVIGHURST, R. J. (1976) "The relative importance of social class and ethnicity in human development." Human Development 19: 56-64.

HERSKOVITS, M. (1942) The Myth of the Negro Past. New York: Harper & Row.

HORTON, P. and C. HUNT (1964) Sociology: New York: McGraw-Hill.

KARENGA, M. (1978) Essays on Struggle: Position and Analysis. San Diego: Kawaida.

KARENGA, M. (1980) Kawaida Theory: An Introductory Outline. Inglewood, CA: Kawaida.

KOCHMAN, T. (1981) Black and White Styles in Conflict. Chicago: Univ. of Chicago Press.

LOMOTEY, K. (1985) "Black principals in black schools: school leadership and school success." Dissertation Abstracts International 46: 2150A. (University Microfilms No. 85-22190, 229)

MacLENNAN, B. W. (1975) "The personalities of group leaders: implications for selecting and training." Int. J. of Group Psychology 25: 177-183.

MONTEIRO, T. (1977) "Ethnicity and the perceptions of principals." Integrated Education 15: 15-16.

MURNANE, R. J. (1975) The Impact of School Resources on the Learning of Inner City Children. Cambridge, MA: Ballinger.

MYRDAL, G. (1944) An American Dilemma: The Negro Problem and Modern Democracy. New York: Harper.

PARKER, W. S., Jr. (1976) "Black-white differences in leadership behavior related to subordinates' reactions." J. of Applied Psychology 61: 140-147.

PINKNEY, A. (1976) Red, Black, and Green. New York: Cambridge Univ. Press.

RIST, R. (1973) The Urban School: A Factory of Failure. Cambridge: MIT Press.

ROGERS, E. M. and F. F. SHOEMAKER (1971) Communication of Innovation: A Cross-Cultural Approach. New York: Free Press.

SARASON, S. ( 1973) "Jewishness, blackishness and the nature-nurture controversy." Amer. Psychologist 28: %2-971.

SOWELL, T. (1981) Ethnic America: A History. New York: Basic Books.

SPADY, W. (1973) "The impact of school resources on students," in F. N. Kerlinger (ed.) Review of Research in Education-I. Itasca, IL: F. E. Peacock.

STODOLSKY, S. S. and G. S. LESSER (1967) "Learning patterns in the disadvantaged." Harvard Educ. Rev. 37: 546-593.

WILSON, W. J. (1980) The Declining Significance of Race: Blacks and Changing American Institutions. Chicago: Univ. of Chicago Press.

## Discussion Questions

1. Discuss the significance of culture as it relates to student success in school. To what extent, if at all, is it necessary to be cognizant of—and focus upon—the culture of students in the teaching/learning process?

2. Discuss your thoughts on the existence of differences in educational leadership styles, based upon race—if there are any.

## References

Brookover, W., & Lezotte, L. (1979). *Changes in school characteristics coincident with changes in student achievement* (Occasional Paper No. 17). Institute for Research on Teaching, College of Education, Michigan State University.

Brookover, W., Schweitzer, J. H., Schneider, J. M., Beady, C.H., Flood, P. K., & Wisenbaker, J. M. (1978). Elementary school climate and school achievement. *American Educational Research Journal, 15*(2), 301–318.

Edmonds, R. (1979). Effective schools for the urban poor. *Educational Leadership, 37*(1), 15–24.

Frederiksen, J. (1975). *School effectiveness and equality of educational opportunity*. Center for Urban Studies, Harvard University.

Rist, R. (1973). *The urban school: A factory for failure*. MIT Press.

# 3.

# AFRICAN AMERICAN PRINCIPALS: BUREAUCRAT/ADMINISTRATORS AND ETHNO-HUMANISTS[1]

*The ethno-humanism role identity is comprised of confidence, commitment, and compassion. I initially observed and described these three traits in three successful principals that I studied (Lomotey, 1985). I further explored these qualities two years later (Lomotey, 1987), and again in another three years (Lomotey, 1990). It would be eight years before I would group these characteristics and refer to them collectively as the ethno-humanist role identity (Lomotey, 1993). In the 1993 article reprinted for this chapter, I describe the ethno-humanist role identity in detail and introduce another role identity: the bureaucrat/administrator role identity—also derived from characteristics portrayed by the more successful Black principals in my earlier work. This reprinted article offers the results of a subsequent study of two successful Black principals, illustrating how they displayed the two role identities: ethno-humanism and bureaucrat/administrator.*

*In the article reprinted in this chapter (Lomotey, 1993), I described the bureaucrat/administrator role identity as follows: "Its objective is meeting societal goals. The principals are merely committed to facilitating the movement of their students from grade to grade. In doing so, they perpetuate the stratification and credentialing functions of schooling" (p. 397). In this same article (Lomotey, 1993), I explain the uniqueness of the ethno-humanist role identity. In this role, principals*

---

1.  REPRINT Lomotey, K. (1993). African American principals: Bureaucrat/administrators and ethno-humanists. *Urban Education, 27*(4), 395–412.

*identify with African-American students as a member of their culture. They argue that academic success is not enough. What is needed, these principals contend, is an education about one's culture, about life, and about where these African-American students fit in the society and in the world. In essence, these leaders encourage African-American students to look at the world through an African-centered set of lenses that provides them with vision that is more focused, has a wider periphery, and more depth (p. 397).*

*In his influential work, Shujaa (1994) makes a distinction between schooling and education. Schooling is the perpetuation of the bureaucracy—the status quo. Education is having one's learning embedded in their own cultural orientation. In this way, they learn about themselves, their people, and the relationship between their people and other people in the world. I argue that the bureaucrat/administrator role identity (goal development, energy harnessing, communication facilitation, and instructional leadership) would perpetuate* schooling; *the ethno-humanist role identity (confidence, commitment, and confidence) would reinforce* education.

*Enjoy.*

# AFRICAN-AMERICAN PRINCIPALS
Bureaucrat/ Administrators
and Ethno-Humanists

*KOFI LOMOTEY*
*Louisiana State University*

*In this article, the author looks at a subset of the data from a study that focused on teachers' responses to a curriculum innovation and conduct an analysis of it that illustrates the differences that distinguish the bureaucrat/ administrator role from the ethno-humanist role as two African-American principals describe how they go about their work. These differences represent a focus on the goals of schooling and on the goals of education. The author found that the principals often moved back and forth between these two identities. They were rarely focusing only on the bureaucrat/administrator role or only on the ethno-humanist role. This overlap of roles, and the tensions between them are reflected throughout the interview transcripts.*

I have been concerned for some time with the academic disenfranchisement of African-American students on all schooling levels (Lomotey, 1990). Regardless of the measures employed (e.g., standardized achievement tests, high school completion rates, suspension rates, special education placement, etc.), on average, African-American students fare poorly when compared to their European-American peers.

Moreover, I am interested in improving the life chances of African-American people, in general (Lomotey & Staley, 1990). Although it is not true that schooling is the "great equalizer" or the answer to all oppression in American society, it is true that improved schooling will increase the likelihood for individuals and groups to improve their status and make greater contributions to their communities and to the society at large.

---

AUTHOR'S NOTE: *I would like to thank Lucille Teichert, a graduate student in the Graduate School of Education (GSE) at the State University of New York at Buffalo (SUNYAB ), for her assistance with the reanalysis of the data employed in this article. I would also like to thank Dianne L. H. Marie, another graduate student in the GSE at SUNYAB, for her comments on an earlier draft of this article.*

There is evidence to suggest that principal leadership is significant in bringing about greater success in school for African-American students. In an earlier study (Lomotey, 1989a), I identified four qualities exhibited by principals in effective schools. These include (a) developing goals; (b) harnessing energy; (c) facilitating communication; and (d) managing instruction, which incorporates teacher supervision, curriculum development, and achievement evaluation.

In this article, I will refer to these qualities to describe what I call the principal's "bureaucrat/administrator" role identity. They are linked to academic success for students and these qualities also help to facilitate the socialization function of schooling in the United States. In addition to influencing the probability of academic success among students, these qualities are also effective in enabling principals to help these students move through the educational hierarchy. Clearly, principals play a major role in enabling schools to serve their sorting, stratification, and credentialing function within the American social system (Bowles & Gintis, 1976; Fine, 1991; Hill, 1989).

I have also identified three qualities shared by some African-American principals in predominantly African-American schools. These are commitment to the education of all students; confidence in the ability of all students to do well; and compassion for, and understanding of, all students and the communities in which they live (Lomotey, 1989a). Herein, I refer to these attributes to describe what I have termed the principal's "ethno-humanist role identity." These principals are not only concerned with the students progressing from grade to grade; they are also concerned with the individual life chances of their students and with the overall improvement of the status of African-American people. This commitment evolves from the cultural affinity that these individuals feel toward African-American students.

I have borrowed the concept of role identity from the symbolic interactionist literature. Roles are determined by the nature of the shared structured relationships that exist between human beings. Individuals may have as many different role identities as there are different kinds of structured social interactions in which they are involved (see Stryker, 1980, pp. 51-65). In this particular discussion, my intent is to describe two distinct role identities that can be detected in the perceptions of African-American principals as they describe their relationships with African-American students. It is my contention that African-American principals often perform their bureaucrat/administrative roles. However, in addition, when they view their African-American culture as a significant bond with their students, they assume ethno-humanist roles. The affinity associated with this second role identity is facilitated, in part, by what political scientists refer to as "homophily"—the notion that people with homogeneous beliefs, values, and cultural attributes tend to interact and communicate more effectively with each other (Rogers & Shoemaker, 1971).

The bureaucrat/administrator role identity facilitates what Shujaa (in press) refers to as "schooling." Its objective is meeting societal goals. The principals are merely committed to facilitating the movement of their students from grade to grade. In so doing, they perpetuate the stratification and credentialing functions of schools.

The ethno-humanist role identity is more appropriately associated with Shujaa's notion of "education." Its objective is meeting a set of cultural goals. In this role, principals identify with African-American students as a member of their culture. They argue that academic success is not enough. What is needed, these principals contend, is an education about one's culture, about life and about where these African-American students fit in the society and in the world. In essence, these leaders encourage African-American students to look at the world through an African-centered set oflenses that provides them with vision that is more focused, has a wider periphery and more depth.

This notion of education, I would argue, has been missing, for the most part, from the experiences afforded the large majority of African-American students in public schools. The result has been generations of African-American students with little sense of identity, purpose, or direction and with little knowledge of the relationship between their schooling and what will occur in their later life (Fine, 1991; Karenga, 1984; Lomotey, 1989b, 1992). In this article, I look at a subset of the data from a study (Shujaa, 1991) that focused on teachers' responses to a curriculum innovation and conduct as analysis of it that illustrates the differences that distinguish the bureaucrat/administrator role from the ethno-humanist role as two African-American principals describe how they go about their work. These differences represent a focus on the goals of schooling on the one hand, and on the goals of education, on the other hand.

## THE ORIGINAL STUDY

Shujaa's (1991) study was conducted in the Buffalo (New York) Public Schools, where an African and African-American curriculum content infusion project was being implemented referred to as the Curriculum Integration Project (CIP). His data were collected at two schools selected by district administrators as pilot sites. The study was-guided by three questions:

1. To what extent did teachers' perceptions of their role in the implementation of African and African-American curriculum content innovations match district policy goals?

2. What differences existed among teachers in the way they interpreted the task of infusing African and African-American curriculum content?

3. What differences existed among teachers' perceptions of the value to students of infusing African and African-American curriculum content?

The study was qualitative and the methods employed included in-depth interviews, document analysis, and observation. Twenty-three interviews were conducted with teachers, principals, and other staff in both schools. Both sites were elementary schools in predominantly African-American communities with overwhelmingly African-American student populations. Whereas Shujaa was primarily interested in teachers' responses to CIP, my concern is with principal leadership as it relates to CIP. I, therefore, focus solely on the two principal interviews for this analysis. I refer to the two principals—both of whom were African—American females as Ms. Grey and Ms. Scarlet.

# DATA ANALYSIS

The analysis is presented in two major parts. I share examples of comments from the principals that characterize both the bureaucrat/administrator role and ethno-humanist role identities. I found that the principals often moved back and forth between these two identities. They were rarely focusing only on the bureaucrat/administrator role or only on the ethno-humanist role. This overlap of roles, and the tensions between them are reflected throughout the interview transcripts.

## THE BUREAUCRAT/ADMINISTRATOR ROLE IDENTITY: PURSUING THE GOALS OF SCHOOLING

### GOAL DEVELOPMENT

Leaders in successful organizations facilitate the development of easily understood and readily applied organizational goals. Moreover, these leaders accept and personify these goals. In schools, such an emphasis by principals helps to facilitate the principal-teacher interaction necessary for greater student success (Castetter, 1976). Clear goals minimize the likelihood of conflicts and misunderstandings among the staff. If principals facilitate and embody clear goals, the likelihood is greater that other members of the organization will internalize these goals (Lomotey, 1989a), thereby increasing the probability of greater organizational harmony.

The principals in this study understood, articulated, and internalized a set of goals related to the infusion project. In doing so, they demonstrated qualities that characterize effective school leaders. Ms. Grey, in explaining her understanding of the project said:

> I understand the goals of the project as to present a more real life history for young people as it portrays the role of their culture in the making of our country and the world. It gives them a sense of identity.

She went on to say that she envisioned the goals being achieved "by sensitizing the staff to include in their daily activities, where appropriate, positive aspects of Black culture and how it relates to the rest of the world."

Ms. Scarlet articulated what she perceived the goals of the infusion project to be when she said:

> I understand the goals to be [to] make the understanding or the knowledge and the awareness of the contributions of African and African-Americans [known] to everybody—all children. . . . The other goal is to sort of fill in the gaps [in the] textbooks and the curriculum that we have been taught.

These comments indicate that the principals held distinct views about the goals of the infusion project. And, as illustrated by Ms. Grey's remarks, there is some evidence that they also understood the significance of articulating these goals clearly to their staff-a process of particular importance to energy harnessing, which is discussed in the next section.

The principals also demonstrated an internalization of the project goals. For instance, Ms. Grey commented, "I bought into the project. . . . [I feel] very strong [about principals giving leadership to this project]. The principal is the leader of the building; [the principal] sets the tone."

## Energy Harnessing

Cooperation is the key to the effective operation of any organization. Such cooperation among staff members in schools can only come about when principals are able to capture the energies of their teachers and encourage them to work toward collectively agreedon goals (Castetter, 1976; McGregor, 1966; Louis & Miles, 1990). Increased staff harmony translates into higher levels of student success.

The principals in this study understood the importance of harnessing the energies of their teachers. Ms. Scarlet expressed the following perception:

> I'm more concerned about my teachers at this point than I am for my kids, because I think if l can win the teachers over, they can set the examples the kids will follow. . . . If the teachers buy into the program, [if] they become enthusiastic about teaching about these different things that they should be teaching, then the kids will learn too.

Ms. Grey added, "When I see my teachers get interested in something and [I observe] the spirit in which they do it and the reaction of the kids, we've met a goal." In each instance, the principals described their perceptions of focusing the energies of their teachers.

Perhaps, most importantly, these principals reflected an understanding that they were working with teachers who possessed varied perspectives and levels of consciousness regarding the infusion project. Although some teachers may have been thoroughly committed to the project, others failed to acknowledge its significance. And, of course, there were others who fit somewhere in between. In describing her perceptions of these differences that teachers brought to the situation, Ms. Grey said:

> It is one thing to do the lesson activities for young people. How teachers present and what prejudices they bring to that presentation can [make it] backfire. Something that can be

very positive can be very negative. What we do is bring to it our own feelings and most people are not really objective enough . . . in our teaching because we personalize things as we see them.

Ms. Scarlet also discussed her perceptions of the varying levels of consciousness that teachers possess:

There are some teachers [whose] children treat each other with the utmost respect. You take these same children somewhere else, and if the environment is not the same, these same children who know how to treat one another so nicely in this environment will follow the path of another. Then you say, well, my goals haven't been met. That is not the children so much as it is the person that is doing the instructing.

At another point, Ms. Scarlet provided additional insight into the staff development implications of teacher differences:

Teachers are not born—they are made. Many teachers, as much as we hate to admit it sometimes, are not very creative. They are [a] regular, average, run-of-the-mill group. Many of them need direction, guidance, aid, and some suggestions. Once they get that, and once they feel that this is going to be a goal, then they begin to buy into it.

Here, Ms. Scarlet is not only revealing her perceptions of the differences among teachers; she is also talking about how she attempts to "bring teachers around" in an effort to have everyone working toward the same set of goals.

Beyond understanding the importance of harnessing the energies of their teachers, Ms. Grey and Ms. Scarlet were both actively engaged in focusing the energies of their faculties toward pursuing the goals of the infusion project. They were also aware of what it takes to harness the energies of teachers. Ms. Scarlet described

## AFRICAN AMERICAN PRINCIPALS

further how she works with teachers who display a low level of commitment to the project:

> I have negative people on our staff. I won't say I don't. We know who these people are and what the rest of us do is try and say something—to be as positive as we can to counteract that. I think that has a lot to do with the success of the program. You don't let certain things stop you. You don't waste your time trying to fight it. You simply work around [it] and you shore up those edges and give those kids a little more exposure and a little more experience in a round about way rather than trying to make an enemy out of someone and then spend all your time fighting.

At another point she expressed the following optimism:

> Because I am positive, I am finding that my teachers now are becoming a little bit more positive. I do a lot of stroking and a lot of telling people that they are doing a good job and encouraging them. I am very careful of when I say things to people, not only what I say.

Ms. Grey discussed another perception of an advantage of the project in harnessing the energy of some teachers:

> I think what [the project] says to that person who doesn't see a need to teach African history or anything about Black people [is that] if they start to look at their own culture, [which] a lot of them don't know about, and see the importance, they will also begin to see the importance of someone else's culture.

## Communication Facilitation

Developing goals and harnessing the energy of staff, although critically important, will only be minimally effective if the principals cannot develop and implement effective two-way communication with their staff. Two-way communication is critical. Many principals communicate with their staffs, but equally important is the degree to which teachers feel comfortable communicating with the principals on matters related to the school's goals. Research has demonstrated a link between effective two-way communication within schools and higher levels of student success (Wellisch, MacQueen, Carriere, & Duck, 1978). The principals in this study have developed effective two-way communication vehicles. Ms. Scarlet spoke about the importance of two-way communication in the school:

> With the African infusion project, I think once we get back into the in-services, once the teachers start working on a day-to-day basis, once the coordinators have materials that they can share with the teachers, they can sit down and discuss. Okay, this is great. I can try this; we are doing a unit next week; let's see if we can give some direction. . . . I think they'll fall into line. [Whereas] if you give it to them and say: I got this at the in-service the other day and maybe you can use it, yeah, they may not look at it again for the next two weeks.

At another point, Ms. Scarlet voiced the following perception of changes she had made that were brought about by the implementation of the project:

> I've learned about people. I believed before, but I know now that some of these people have to be handled a little bit differently. For example, my coordinator becomes fierce about a lot of things and what she's beginning to see is that . . . you are emotional about a lot of things and there is nothing wrong with that. But you have to get beyond that because

# AFRICAN AMERICAN PRINCIPALS

these people over here need to see and understand that this is something they need. They may not want it, but they need it. Rather than get ornery about it, you have to understand that they are frightened; their whole life is shaken up; and that's good; and they retaliate and you have to be secure enough yourself to know this.

In the above statement, Ms. Scarlet is emphasizing the importance of effective two-way communication, but here again, implications for one's ability to harness the energy of teachers are evident. Principals must not only be aware of the varying levels of consciousness that teachers possess; they must also respond appropriately.

Ms. Scarlet expressed her perceptions of the effects of communication on staff morale: "Once we start this in-service and not just lecture but actually . . . talk about different kinds of things and break up into groups and have discussions and share ideas . . . then you'll get more enthusiasm."

In describing her perceptions of what teachers are doing differently and how their attitudes have begun to change as a result of the project, Ms. Grey said, "They communicate that to me." She went on at another point to discuss her perceptions of an increased level of communication among the teachers, brought about by the implementation of the project:

[Since the implementation of the infusion project] there's been a lot of debate. . . . What you see is teachers who debate whether we should be doing this. At least they're talking. It's not under the ground or under the cover that nobody talks about it. . . . I think there are some other people who use this to say to people, "What are you doing about it?"

Ms. Scarlet described how she communicated with teachers about the decision to introduce CIP at their school: "We were told in June of last year that we were going to be a pilot and I had a faculty meeting and we talked about it. I told them how I felt." Here she reflected an understanding of the importance of free and open communication with her staff.

## INSTRUCTIONAL MANAGEMENT

Principals in successful schools demonstrate instructional management that includes curriculum planning, teacher supervision, and achievement evaluation. These leaders often participate actively in staff meetings and other aspects of the curriculum planning process (California State Department of Education, 1977). They are also involved on a regular basis in the supervision of teachers, often through regular observations (Wellisch et al., 1978). Finally, principals who are instructional leaders play a meaningful role in the evaluation of student achievement. This is done through the monitoring of schoolwide test results and through regular evaluative and prescriptive dialogue with teachers (Brookover & Lezotte, 1979).

I will briefly discuss the two principals' perception about curriculum planning and teacher supervision. Because CIP was a relatively new program at the time data were collected, there was no assessment mechanism in place to evaluate student achievement. Accordingly, little, if anything, was said in the interviews by the principals about their roles in the evaluation of student achievement in the CIP program.

### *Curriculum Planning*

With regard to her involvement in curriculum planning, Ms. Grey provided the following comment: "I am searching out new materials and I'm being careful how monies are spent. . . . I have become more aware of what's out there and what's good and what's positive and ways to use it." At another point, she described another aspect of her input into the curriculum planning process: "I did something different last year. I said to them: Let's do an international thing. Let's have lots of countries, lots of people . . . choose your country. They liked that. . . . And the kids had to go and do the research."

Ms. Scarlet also stressed the importance of her involvement in curriculum matters: "[My teachers] . . . went to a couple of inservices in June and I went too. I think it is important as far as my role goes to participate along with the staff. . . . I intend to continue to do that." Each of these principals understood the importance of their hands-on involvement in curriculum planning.

### Teacher Supervision

Ms. Scarlet's perception of the importance of teacher supervision is emphasized in the following comments:

> People lose their enthusiasm because they don't have that enthusiasm in a big way. What gets measured gets done. When you stop measuring it, they slide back. Not because maybe they don't buy into the program, but because there are other things that become priority and they don't know how to make this infusion project a part of those priorities.

Ms. Scarlet also spoke about another aspect of her teacher supervision responsibilities—monitoring and feedback. She stated, "I do check lesson plans and notice when teachers have put some things in writing. I write a little note and tell them, 'I see you are using African culture.' "

To summarize, the above analyses illustrate how these principals perceive their bureaucrat/administrator role identities. The assumption of role identities by African-American leaders serves a critical function in maintaining the status quo in our schools and in our society. Schools impart information, instill values, and control people (Lomotey & Brookins, 1988) and school leaders help to facilitate these functions by serving in the roles of bureaucrats/administrators.

## THE ETHNO-HUMANIST ROLE IDENTITY: PURSUING THE GOALS OF EDUCATION

Achieving a significant improvement in the level of African-American student success in public schools and in the life chances of African-American people will require a greater focus on these students by school leaders. This increased focus must be geared toward enabling these students to feel good about themselves and about their people. Moreover, these students must be encouraged to expand their worldviews and to learn to see the world through the eyes of Africans.

The perpetuation of African-American culture requires this redirection in the education of African-American students. African-American school leaders play a key role in bringing about these changes. Commitment to the education of all students, compassion and understanding of students and their communities, and confidence in their skill, are necessary components of this critical change effort. I will discuss how each of these attributes were evidenced in the attitudes of these two African-American principals.

### COMMITMENT

Both of these principals expressed their commitment to the education of African-American children. As they discussed the need for the infusion project, they recalled the lack of African-American content in their own schooling and that of their students' parents. They noted the difference between education in the northern and southern United States, and they stressed the significance of African-American churches and colleges in disseminating African and African-American history and culture.

Ms. Grey believed that the infusion project would not work for African-American students, or for any students, unless all educators—and not just African-American educators—were involved in the project: "I think . . . that there needs to be some kind of pressure or monitoring of principals and their attitude and it should not be up to Black teachers or Black principals to carry out such a project."

# AFRICAN AMERICAN PRINCIPALS

Her concerns about the success of the project emanated from her perception of systemic problems in the American educational system and its treatment of African and African-American history and culture: "I think we have to go back to the teacher training institutions. It's got to be included. . . . They've got to be sensitized. It doesn't matter where you teach, you need to do it in a sensitive kind of way." Regarding the significance of the project, she added:

> [This project) is a beginning. There should never be an end. While there are people and racism, it should always be a part. It should not be related to money. We don't teach reading because of money. We don't teach math because of money. We teach it because we feel it is important that we know how to read and how to do math. It is also important that we know about people and it should be considered like that.

These statements reveal Ms. Grey's deep-felt commitment to her people—a feeling that goes much deeper than that required by her bureaucrat/administrator role identity.

## COMPASSION

Ms. Scarlet's compassionate understanding of African-American children is articulated in the following statements:

> I am interested in children learning and knowing information, but I think we need to have our children understand where we come from. Our people are able to deal with conflict, have an inner dignity and know how to cope with situations. Many of our kids have lost that. I grew up learning that; my grandmother taught me. I think a lot of us grew up that way. What I am seeing now, somewhere in these past 20 years or so, we have lost that with our kids; we don't know how to deal with adversity; we don't know how to deal with problems; we don't know how to be adults

and get along in the world; and I think that if teachers are able to learn from reading in the African cultures that will give them another vehicle. Maybe having an additional wealth of information that you can tell children to help them understand how to deal with problems, how to relate to themselves and growing up [will help].

This statement, perhaps better than any from the data, captures the essence of the notion of the ethno-humanist role identity. Ms. Scarlet's compassion comes through as she personalizes the education of African-American students. Her recounting of what learning from her grandmother about African-American people was like and the need for such experiences to begin with today's African-American youth reflect this compassion. Implicit in this understanding is the acknowledgment of the importance of the transmission of a culture—in this case, African-American culture-from one generation to another. More evidence of Ms. Scarlet's compassion and of her immersion in African-American culture comes through in her constant inclusionary use of the term "we." She says, "We have lost that with our kids . . . "; "we don't know how to deal with adversity . . . "; and "we don't know how to be adults."

In stressing the importance of the infusion project, Ms. Grey displayed her compassion and understanding: "[I believe this project is needed] because I came up through a system in Buffalo where we were not a part of the history of the majority of things that were taught in the school settings." Further evidence of Ms. Grey's compassion and understanding was apparent when she talked about African-American teenagers growing up unaware of their history or the current reality of racism. She noted that they are not prepared for the problems they will face once they grow up. She said, "They don't understand racism; that's why they have the problems they are having. That's why a lot of them don't hang in there. . . . Nowhere were they told about it; so they run into problems they can't handle."

Involvement with implementing the infusion project itself was credited with fostering the development of at least one of the

AFRICAN AMERICAN PRINCIPALS

principals' sense of compassion and understanding. In this regard, Ms. Grey commented, "[Since the project] I think I am more aware [of kids], and I make sure I'm positive to a child."

## CONFIDENCE

Ms. Scarlet's confidence was reflected in her understanding of the potential impact of the project on her students:

> My goal for this building is to have these children learn and grow and develop and be everything that they can possibly be. I think that if the African infusion program is done right, it is a vehicle by which the children will learn about themselves and want to be able to achieve.

This statement, although reflecting Ms. Scarlet's confidence and her deep ethno-humanism, also shows, at times, how much these school leaders' bureaucrat/administrator and ethno-humanist role identities overlap. While discussing the impact of the project on African-American youth, Ms. Scarlet is at the same time articulating school goals.

In summary, both of the principals in this study played their bureaucrat/administrator roles well. However, they were also concerned about equally important "education" issues related to the holistic development of their students. They wanted to ensure that their students had every opportunity to learn about African and African-American history and culture and they wanted their students to develop positive self-concepts and generally to feel good about themselves and their people. Moreover, they wanted the students to develop a love for and a commitment to African-American people. They were committed to the education of their students; they were confident that these children could do well; and they displayed compassion for, and understanding of the children and the communities in which they lived. In sum, these African-American school leaders were committed to doing their part to insure the perpetuation of African-American culture.

## CONCLUSION

Principals are indeed administrators and their behavior reflects this truism. But a principal is also a member of a cultural group (e.g., African-American culture, Hispanic-American culture, European-American culture). Moreover, if principals view their cultures as significant, they consciously or unconsciously make a distinction between their bureaucrat/administrator role and ethno-humanist function. This was the case with the two African-American principals observed in the present study. Although they demonstrated goal development, energy harnessing, communication facilitation, and instruction management, they also demonstrated commitment to their students, compassion for their students, and confidence in their students. Consequently, but not at all unexpectedly, the personal (ethno-humanist) and professional (bureaucrat/administrator) role identities were often intertwined.

Ms. Scarlet, in discussing the infusion project, said, "[It is intended to] make all children . . . [and] all teachers . . . more aware of our contribution to the American culture. That's one of the goals." While Ms. Scarlet is describing one of the goals of the program (schooling) in this statement, she is, at the same time, personalizing the goal when she says "our contribution." She is making a connection between what African-American children do in school and how it affects their lives outside of school.

At another point, Ms. Scarlet further articulated her perceptions of the goals of the project:

> One of the goals is to help African-American children develop a sense of self-esteem so that they realize that they have a place in this world culture in addition to the United States culture. I think those are the broad goals of the program—not only for us but also for the majority population. So things have been rather one-sided and I think one of the goals is to show that all of us have worked together and contributed to make this world what it is.

Here again, her comments offer a clear discussion of the goals, but she also adds a more personal and cultural "editorial." She is assessing the shortcomings of the status quo and arguing that a new agenda is necessary in schools in order to insure the success of African-American students.

The ability to strike a balance between schooling and education is essential in order for public school educators to educate African-American students effectively. Although it is critically important that we improve the academic achievement of African-American students, it is equally important that we enable these students to fit into and serve a meaningful role in the African-American community and in the United States. Moreover, African-American students need to be made to feel good about themselves as individuals and as African-Americans. Presently, many of these students see little connection between their educational experiences and their later lives. Moreover, they are not developing a commitment to the development of their own communities. Only with a greater emphasis from school leaders (teachers and administrators) on education for African-American students will we begin to see a qualitative change in the life chances of African-American people. African-American school leaders must take the lead in this by accentuating their ethno-humanist role identities.

## *References*

Bowles, S., & Gintis, H. (1976). *Schooling in capitalist America.* New York: Basic Books.

Brookover, W. B., & Lezotte, L. W. (1979). *Changes in school characteristics coincident with changes in student achievement.* East Lansing: Michigan State University, College of Urban Development.

California State Department of Education. (1977). *1977 California school effectiveness study. The first year: 1974-75.* Sacramento, CA: California State Department of Education, Office of Program Evaluation and Research.

Castetter, W. B. (1976). *The personnel function in educational administration.* New York: Macmillan.

Fine, M. (1991). *Framing dropouts: Notes on the politics of an urban public high school.* Albany, NY: State University of New York Press.

Hill, K. G. (1989, March). *Grade retention and dropping out of school.* Paper presented at the annual meeting of the American Educational Research Association, San Francisco, CA.

Karenga, M. (1984). *Introduction to Black studies.* Los Angeles: Kawaida.

Lomotey, K. (1989a). *African-American principals: School leadership and success.* Westport, CT: Greenwood.

Lomotey, K. (1989b). Cultural diversity in the school: Implications for principals. *NASSP Bulletin, 73*(521), 81-88.

Lomotey, K. (1990). Introduction. In K. Lomotey (Ed.), *Going to school: The African-American experience* (pp. 1-9). Albany, NY: State University of New York Press.

Lomotey, K. (1992). Independent Black institutions: African-centered education models. *Journal of Negro Education, 61,* 455-462.

Lomotey, K., & Brookins, C. (1988). The independent Black institutions: A cultural perspective. In D. T. Slaughter & D. J. Johnson (Eds.), *Visible now: Blacks in private schools* (pp. 163-183). Westport, CT: Greenwood.

Lomotey, K., & Staley, J. (1990). The education of African-Americans in the Buffalo public schools. In H. Taylor (Ed.), *African Americans and the rise of Buffalo's post-industrial city, 1940 to present, Vol. 2* (pp. 157-186). Buffalo, NY: Buffalo Urban League.

Louis, K. S., & Miles, M. B. (1990). *Improving the urban high school: What works and why.* New York: Teachers College Press.

McGregor, D. (1966). *Leadership and motivation.* Cambridge, MA: MIT Press.

Rogers, E. M., & Shoemaker, F. F. (1971). *Communication of innovation: A cross-cultural approach.* New York: Free Press.

Shujaa, M. J. (1991). *Teacher's responses to the implementation of an African-American curriculum content infusion policy. Final report.* Unpublished manuscript, State University of New York at Buffalo, Graduate School of Education, Buffalo.

Shujaa, M. J. (Ed.). (in press). *Too much schooling, too little education: A paradox of African-American life.* Trenton, NJ: Africa World Press.

Stryker, S. (1980). *Symbolic interactionism.* Menlo Park, CA: Benjamin/ Cummings.

Wellisch, J.B., MacQueen, A.H., Carriere, R. A., & Duck, G. A. ( 1978). School management and organization in successful schools. *Sociology of Education, 51*, 211-226.

---

## *Discussion Questions*

1. Discuss the leadership of principals with whom you are familiar, in the context of their displaying the ethno-humanist role identity (i.e., confidence, commitment, and compassion). Consider how, if at all, they display this role identity. How would you display this role identity?

2. Discuss the leadership of principals with whom you are familiar, in the context of their displaying the bureaucrat/ administrator role identity (i.e., goal development, energy harnessing, communication facilitation, and instructional leadership). Consider how, if at all, they display this role identity. How would you display this role identity?

3. Consider your views on the significance of principal leadership for the academic, social, cultural, and spiritual success of students. To what extent—and in what ways—are the leadership qualities of principals important for the overall success of students?

## *References*

Lomotey, K. (1985). *Black principals in Black schools: Implication for school success.* Dissertation Abstracts International 46: 2150A (University Microfilms No. 85-22190, 229).

Lomotey, K. (1987). Black principals for Black students: Some preliminary observations. *Urban Education, 22*(2), 173–181.

Lomotey, K. (1990). Qualities shared by African-American principals in effective schools: A preliminary analysis. In K. Lomotey (Ed.), *Going to school: The African-American experience* (pp. 180–195). SUNY Press.

Lomotey, K. (1993). African American principals: Bureaucrat/administrators and ethno-humanists. *Urban Education, 27*(4), 395–412.

Shujaa, M. J. (1994). *Too much schooling, too little education: A paradox of African American Life.* Africa World Press.

# PART TWO:
## Issues of Gender

4.

# RESEARCH ON THE LEADERSHIP OF BLACK WOMEN PRINCIPALS: IMPLICATIONS FOR BLACK STUDENTS[1]

*In 2018, I conducted a literature review of the leadership of Black women principals. The review was published the following year in the journal* Educational Researcher *(Lomotey, 2019). To my knowledge, this was the first published literature review on the leadership of Black women principals.*

*I noted during the process that there are significantly more Black women principals than there are Black male principals in U.S. public schools. In 2018, there were 6,755 Black women principals and only 3,391 Black male principals—a difference of nearly two to one (U.S. Equal Employment Opportunity Commission, 2018). This post-*Brown *comparison between the number of Black women principals and the number of Black male principals is in sharp contrast to the comparison pre-*Brown. *Surprisingly, however, there was a significant number of Black women principals pre-*Brown, *many of whom played a substantial role as school leaders. According to Tillman (2004):*

African American women also played exemplary roles in the education of Blacks in the pre-*Brown* era (Alston & Jones, 2002; Franklin, 1990; Hines & Thompson, 1998; Jones, 2003;

---

1.  REPRINT Lomotey, K. (2019). Research on the leadership of Black women principals: Implications for Black students. *Educational Researcher 48*(6), 336–348.

Perkins, 1987). Educated African American women opened schools in the North and the South and served as teachers and principals. Jeanes Supervisors were female principals who served as teachers and principals from 1907 through 1967. (p. 108)

*At another point, Tillman provides an example, "Sarah Smith was named principal of the African School in Brooklyn, New York, in 1863 and was the first African American female principal in the New York public school system" (p. 108).*

*Dunbar (2015) chimes in with the following confirmation of the significant roles that Black women played as school leaders pre-*Brown:

History touts the accomplishments of African American female leaders both before and after the *Brown v. Board of Education* Supreme Court ruling. Pioneers such as Sarah Smith, Mary McLeod Bethune, Fannie Jackson Coppin, and several others have been credited for not only fighting against the inequalities that existed for students, but also for paving the way for teachers and educational leaders both past and present to experience a more equitable educational space. (p. 21)

*I reprint that 2019 article on the leadership of Black women principals here. In Chapter 5, I introduce a new—previously unpublished—literature review focusing on the leadership of Black male principals.*

*Enjoy!*

# RESEARCH ON THE LEADERSHIP OF BLACK WOMEN PRINCIPALS: IMPLICATIONS FOR BLACK STUDENTS

*KOFI LOMOTEY*

*In this exploratory review, I consider research on Black women principals for the period 1993 to 2017, using 57 research reports obtained from dissertations, journal articles, and a book chapter. This exploration is of particular significance given the continuous disenfranchisement and subsequent underachievement of Black children in U.S. schools and the importance of Black women principals in addressing this quagmire. I highlight the methodological and theoretical traits of these studies, single out overstressed approaches, and highlight the most significant gaps in research on Black women principals. Major findings are (1) the large majority of studies on Black women principals appear in dissertations; (2) researchers studying Black women principals explore the lived experiences of Black women principals (e.g., race, gender) and aspects of the leadership of these women (e.g., transformational leadership); (3) the most common theoretical framework in these studies is Black Feminist Thought, followed by Critical Race Theory and Standpoint Theory; (4) all of the studies employed qualitative methods, while a few also included quantitative methods; (5) the principals who were studied served in elementary, middle, and high schools; and (6) spirituality, race, and gender are important to these leaders. Following a discussion of the findings, I conclude with implications for (1) future research, (2) the preparation of aspiring principals, and (3) the professional development of practicing principals.*

**Keywords:** administration; Black education; descriptive analysis; leadership; principals; survey research

The disenfranchisement of Black children has been persistent, pervasive, and disproportionate since it became legal to educate Black children in the United States; this disenfranchisement has led to widescale underachievement (Heidi, 2005; Holzman, 2012;

Lomotey, 1990; Milner & Howard, 2004; Murrell, 2002). Black children endeavor to achieve in school but are constantly thwarted by educational inequities and achievement and opportunity gaps (Milner, 2010, 2012).

The most significant relationship in schools is between the teacher and the student; this is where "the rubber meets the road." If Black children are to reach their full potential, we must positively impact the teacher/student relationship. Still, with a culturally responsive orientation, principals can make a difference. More specifically, Black principals can play a unique role in increasing the success of Black children (Kelley, 2012; Kochman, 1981; MacLennan, 1975; Williams & Loeb, 2012). Quite a bit of research suggests that Black principals make a difference for Black children (Johnson, 2006; Lee, 2007; Reitzug & Patterson, 1998; Tillman, 2004). This view is not counterintuitive, as we know of the significance of what psychologists refer to as homophily: the notion that individuals sharing beliefs, values, qualities, background, or social class are more likely to better communicate and relate to each other (Rogers & Shoemaker, 1971).[1]

The specific—and perhaps unique—impact of Black women principals on the educational experiences of Black children poses many questions one might expect to have been examined during the past 25 years.

Women comprised 54% (N = 49,030) of the principals in U.S. public schools in 2015–16. There were 6,340 Black women principals—13% of the total number of women principals and nearly twice the number of Black male principals (N = 3,210). Nearly 40% of Black women principals are under the age of 45. The plurality of Black women principals have served as principals for between four and nine years. Nearly one half of all Black women principals hold a master's degree, and it is their highest degree. Appendices B, C, and D show the age range of Black women principals, their years of experience, and their educational credentials (National Center for Education Statistics, 2016). I now discuss my rationale for exploring research on Black women principals.

## Why This Line of Inquiry?

Black principals make a difference for Black students, and most Black principals are women. Perhaps most importantly, in the studies of Black women principals that I have uncovered, we hear the voices of Black women—powerful voices that have for far too long been muted. By looking at these studies and hearing the voices of Black women principals, we have a much greater opportunity to understand their leadership—and principal leadership in general. Ultimately, by deconstructing the leadership of these women, we have the opportunity to gain greater insights into the future of (Black women) principal leadership. We can address the all-important question: To what extent has the research of the past 25 years given voice to Black women principals and to what effect? If Black principals can make a difference for Black students, and since there is some research that suggests that men and women principals lead differently (Eagley & Johnson, 1990; Herndon, 2002), it would be important to look at the research—limited as it is—on Black women principals.

Black women principals continue to be oppressed, at least by race and gender (Collins, 2004; hooks, 1981; Shorter-Gooden, 2004). The intersection of these identities is fundamental to their leadership experiences and practices. This is, of course, compounded—for some Black women principals—by their class and/or their age, as classism and ageism rear their ugly heads.

I seek to illuminate characteristics of the leadership of Black women principals that may be of relevance for the preparation and professional development of principals and for further study. I wondered about (1) the predominant research questions asked heretofore; (2) the significance of previous findings for principal leadership—particularly Black women principal leadership; (3) the significance of previous findings for children—particularly Black children; (4) the impact of the leadership of Black women principals; and (5) the impact of race, gender, age, and class on the leadership of Black women principals.

Exploring these issues could have a profound effect on Black women in general and Black women principals in particular. Studying these issues is important because of the ways in which they interact to maintain the oppression of Black women and many groups. Through research that identifies how intersecting issues affect Black women principals, scholars and practitioners may be able to develop new—and adapt current—strategies that could ultimately benefit the schools and students that Black women lead. I next consider the brief history of research on Black women principals.

## The Newness of the Field of Study

For more than 50 years, much has been written about the leadership of White male principals (Lomotey, 1989), but significantly less has been written about other school leaders, and even less has been shared related to Black women principals. When I first wrote about Black principals, there was very little written on these leaders (e.g., Abney, 1980), and there were no studies that had been published specifically about Black women principals. (I am not including here studies of "minority" principals, studies comparing Black and White principals or "thought pieces" on Black principals.)

Over the past 25 or so years, a number of studies have been conducted focusing on Black women principals, primarily in dissertations and to a lesser extent in journals. The first studies that I uncovered were published between 1993 and 1998 (Case, 1997; Dillard, 1995; Lomotey, 1993; Reitzug & Patterson, 1998; Tweedle, 1996). It was not until 2000 that two other studies appeared (Bagwell, 2000; Hobson-Horton, 2000). The Lomotey, Dillard, Case, and Reitzug and Patterson studies were journal articles; the Tweedle, Hobson-Horton, and Bagwell studies were dissertations.

This is the first comprehensive review of research on Black women principals. In it, I seek to further the journey of positioning Black women principals in the struggle to improve the achievement of Black children and to ultimately increase their overall life chances. Black women principals are significantly understudied at

RESEARCH ON THE LEADERSHIP OF BLACK WOMEN PRINCIPALS 61

this point. If, as I suggest, Black principals make a difference for Black children, the work herein is an important step in assessing the potential for increasing the success of Black children. This exploratory review provides the groundwork for future theory-testing studies looking at the leadership of Black women principals. Next, I describe this review.

## The Nature of This Review

In this review, I consider research on Black women principals addressing six fundamental research questions: (1) Where does research on Black women principals appear? That is, where is it published? (2) What do researchers study regarding Black women principals? (3) What theoretical frameworks do researchers employ when studying Black women principals? (4) What research methods do scholars draw upon when studying Black women principals? (5) What levels of leadership (i.e., elementary, middle, and/or high school) are represented in the research on Black women principals? and (6) What are the ultimate findings in studies of Black women principals?

I seek, in part, to provide guidance to researchers in this area. As in most fields, some subareas are saturated, while others are understudied. I include illustrations of areas that are over-studied and point out where critical gaps in the research may exist. The methods that I used are discussed next.

## Methods

### How the Review Was Compiled

Through a thorough scan of the literature, including dissertations, journal articles, and book chapters, the 57 studies reviewed in this article were uncovered. The majority of the publications were secured through the Hunter Library at Western Carolina University in Cullowhee, North Carolina; some materials are held in the Hunter Library, and others were purchased or borrowed through Interlibrary

Loan Services. Substantial assistance was provided by the Library staff, most notably Dr. Beth McDonough, Research & Instruction Librarian. Next, I describe the studies included in this review.

### Included Studies

All of the studies that appear in this comprehensive review were published between 1993 and 2017, a period of 24 years. I found no studies of Black women principals prior to 1993. The largest number of studies (eight or 14%) were published in 2013 followed by those that were inked in 2009 and 2016 (seven studies each) and 2014 (five studies). The sample sizes range from one to 70. (The study that has a sample size of 70 is an outlier. Absent that study, the sample sizes range from one to 14.) A plurality of studies have a sample size of three (18 studies or 32%). The next most common sample sizes are one and six, each with six studies. (See Appendix E.)

All of the studies in this review include samples made up *exclusively* of women principals in the United States who identify as Black, excluding immigrants. Studies that focused on Black women principals outside of the United States were excluded. Immigrants and principals in other countries were excluded because of the potential for conflating data (e.g., cultural realities, geographical particularities). (Several studies were uncovered that were conducted in other countries, including Canada and South Africa [e.g., Armstrong & Mitchell, 2017; Mayienga, 2013].) Also excluded were studies of Black women assistant principals (e.g., Arnold & Brooks, 2013; Best, 2013). This was done because the experiences of assistant principals are very different from those of principals. I did not consider studies that compared the leadership of Black women principals with that of White women principals (e.g., Fortenberry, 1987; Turner, 2004). This is not a comparative review; my goal was to learn about the leadership of Black women principals. Essays on Black women principals were also not considered for this review (e.g., Horsford, 2012). Studies that included in their samples Black women principals and Black women aspiring to become principals were excluded from consideration (e.g., Loder, 2005) and studies that included Black women principals and other building level or district level administrators in their samples were excluded (e.g., Page, 2007). In both instances, I did not want to confound data on different types of leaders. I move now to a discussion of the findings of this review.

## Findings: Characteristics of the Studies

### Research Question #1: Where Does Research of Black Women Principals Appear?

As is the case within the general field of principal leadership, most of the studies of Black women principals appear in dissertations. Forty-three (75%) of the included studies appear in dissertations. Thirteen (23%) of the studies appear in journals, and one study (2%) is published as a book chapter.

### Research Question #2: What Do Researchers Study Regarding Black Women Principals?

I distinguish two types of studies in this review. First are those that pose questions or uncover findings related to the lived experiences (personal attributes and identities) of Black women principals; they deal with the impact of issues such as race, gender, spirituality, and age. The second group of studies addresses questions related to aspects of the leadership of Black women principals (e.g., leadership style and contexts). They address issues such as transformational leadership, leading in urban schools, culturally responsive leadership, and ethno-humanism. The majority of the studies (44 or 77%) address lived experiences—questions related to how the principals cope with certain realities within the principalship (e.g., spirituality, race, gender, and age). The other studies (13 or 23%) tackle questions pertaining to the leadership of principals (e.g., transformational leadership, culturally responsive leadership, and ethno-humanism).

Some themes appear in both types of studies. Nineteen of the studies (33%) raise questions related to race and gender (and sometimes class and age also); 16 of these studies explore the lived experiences of Black women principals. Three focus on aspects of principal leadership.

Spirituality is an area of examination or a finding in 17 (30%) of the studies. Twelve of these 17 studies focus on the lived experiences of Black women principals. The remaining five studies that explore or uncover issues of spirituality are studies of the leadership aspects of Black women principals.

Leading in urban schools is the second most popular focus in these studies of Black women principals. Scholars sought to better understand the impact of the leadership of Black women principals in inner city schools. Urban school leadership is explored in 14 (25%) of the studies; 11 (79%) of these studies pose questions related to the lived experiences of Black women principals. Other aspects of leadership that are explored within urban centers include leading in a predominantly White school, leading in a turnaround school, and displaying transformational leadership.

### *Research Question #3: What Frameworks Do Researchers Employ When Studying Black Women Principals?*

Nearly half of these studies of Black women principals (24 or 42%) use Black Feminist Thought (BFT) as a framework in an attempt to better understand the issues surrounding the leadership of these women. Eleven (19%) use BFT solely as a theoretical framework. Others use it along with Critical Race Theory (CRT) (five or 9%). Still others use BFT in conjunction with Standpoint Theory (ST) (five or 9%). Other frameworks employed include Feminist, Transformational Leadership, Life Course, and Womanist, reflecting a wide variety of inquiry styles.

### *Research Question #4: What Research Methods Are Used in Studying Black Women Principals?*

All of the studies included in this review use qualitative methods. There are three (5%) mixed methods studies, though there are no purely quantitative studies. The most common data collection procedure is interviews: 43 (75%) of the studies use interviews at least in part to collect their data. Twenty-six studies (46%) employ only interviews to collect data. Other data August/September 2019 339 collection strategies employed more than once include observations (14) and document review (five). (See Appendix F.)

### *Research Question #5: What Level(s) of Leadership (i.e., Elementary, Middle, and High School) Are Represented in the Research on Black Women Principals?*

Of the 57 studies included in this review, 26 (46%) include principals on one level only: 15 studies (26%) include elementary school principals only. Ten studies (18%) include high school principals only. Twenty-seven studies (47%) include a combination of principals on two or three levels (i.e., elementary and secondary principals; elementary and middle school principals; middle and high school principals and; elementary, middle, and high school principals). (The level of the principal[s] was not mentioned in four of the studies.) (See Appendix G.)

### *Research Question #6: What Are the Major Findings in Studies of Black Women Principals?*

Research Question #2 focuses on the areas that researchers target when formulating their studies—what areas of the leadership of Black women principals they chose to focus on at the outset. This sixth research question speaks to what the researchers found at the conclusion of their inquiries—what rises to the top as the most significant aspects of the leadership of these women. Researchers in 13 (23%) of the studies found that spirituality was important to the Black women principals whom they studied. Twelve studies show race as a significant factor impacting the leadership of Black women principals. Issues related to gender were a barrier to Black women principals in 10 (18%) of the studies reviewed herein. Other issues that are significant in the findings are that several of the principals (1) displayed and valued passion/mothering/caring (in nine studies), (2) benefitted from mentoring (in six studies), (3) exhibited servant leadership (in six studies), and (4) valued family (in five studies). The valuing of caring is consistent with BFT, which emphasizes the importance of Black women focusing on caring. The acknowledgement of family is consistent with the reliance on spirituality in the Black community, wherein a key component is a focus on family and community. I now turn to a discussion of the most significant findings.

## Discussion: What the Findings Mean

In this section I focus on key findings in four areas: spirituality, urbanicity, theoretical frameworks, and school level; my rationale follows. In these studies, the most often cited characteristic of Black women principals is their spirituality. Most Black children and most Black women principals in these studies are in urban districts. The most widely used frameworks in these studies are BFT, CRT, and ST. My focus on the school level (e.g., elementary) stems in part from the absence of a focus on school level in several of these studies. This is problematic, as there are indeed different issues related to leadership at the elementary, middle, and high school levels.

### Spirituality

The discussion of spirituality in studies of Black women principals is not counterintuitive. This is an important point; spirituality is a major element in the lives of a large number of Black women principals and is fundamental to their leadership (Spicer, 2004). More particularly, they often draw upon their sacred upbringing and their connection to their place of worship in their daily lives. Akin to this connection is a focus on civic responsibility. Indeed, the focus on this Africanism—the centrality of family, community, and spirituality—is essential in the lives of many Black leaders (Shujaa & Shujaa, 2015). They believe that this focus contributes positively to their success in life. Spicer (2004) articulates this truism well.

> Spirituality and religion have long been the "backbone" of the Black family and culture. Throughout history the Black

church has been the central and most powerful institution in the African American community. . . . The African American church stands without challenge as the "cultural womb" of the community (Lincoln and Mamiya, 1990). In an earlier study by Frazier (1962) the Black church was seen as a major influence in African American women's assuming leadership roles and in developing a network of support linked to other networks in the African American community. . . . The role of church and spirituality is significant in understanding the resilience of African American women. (pp. 64–65)

In Tweedle's study (1996), the voice of one of the author's respondents is clear on this matter.

Who I am has totally surpassed the African American woman thing. I'm a child of God and the loyalty that comes from being a child of God, classifying myself as an African American female can't touch that. I feel like I'm led by God. My intrinsic motivation is not based on fear or anxiety or anything like that. I don't feel like I have to prove myself to anyone but God. That's what I'm really striving for. As long as I strive to please him, I'm going to actually surpass what humans expect of me. (p. 159)

The significance of spirituality, or religion, for Black women principals and for Black people in general, is worthy of additional discussion herein.[2] Faith in religion is very strong within the Black community. According to Masci (2018), Black people in the United States are significantly more religious than Whites or Latino/a people. (See Appendix H.) Indeed, church has always been a foundational institution within the Black community since enslavement. For Blacks, spirituality fosters a sense of optimism and offers the promise of survival. It is viewed as a buffer in the midst of institutionalized White racism.

The findings of this review suggest that religion is a fundamental component of the lives of Black women principals. It is, they believe, pivotal to their leadership; they rely on it every day. They credit their religious belief for their achievements. As it relates to their leadership, these women are inspired, motivated, and confident in their responsibilities in part because of their faith in religion. This is consistent with the longstanding religious experiences and beliefs of Black people in the United States (Masci, 2018).

## Urbanicity

As our challenges in education, particularly for Black children, are often centered in urban communities, this is important research. The focus on urban school leadership is also not surprising, as most Black women principals serve in predominantly Black schools and a large number of these schools are in urban areas. Being in urban centers, of course, adds to the challenges of leading these schools, as a myriad of issues are associated with urban communities and accordingly with urban schools. These institutions are often the most difficult to lead, given the less trained teachers, the numerous social and health issues, the revolving door for teachers, and much more, including socioeconomic issues, unemployment issues, the prison pipeline, drugs, and an opportunity gap experienced by students in these schools (Bloom & Erlandson, 2003).

## Theoretical Frameworks

The presumed value of BFT is evident in that four out of every 10 of the studies in this review employ it solely or in part. BFT is valuable because it concentrates on the unique experiences of Black women with a focus on (1) dialogue as a tool for assessing what we know; (2) caring or nurturing, a fundamental characteristic of Black women;[3] and (3) the significance of accountability. Moreover, it was developed by Black women for use in assessing their circumstances (Collins, 2004). This uniqueness and its impact on Black women—and Black people—are alluded to in the words of hooks (1981), "No other group in America has so had their identity socialized out of existence as have Black women" (p. 20). Spicer (2004) adds "[Black women] are rarely recognized as a group separate and distinct from Black men, or as a part of the larger group of 'women' in this culture" (p. 7). BFT facilitates a uniquely feminine, African-centered way of looking at the world.

Perhaps one of the most powerful theories used to assess the experiences of oppressed peoples is CRT, first employed in the study of law (Bell, 1995; Gillbord & Ladson-Billings, 2009; Ladson-Billings, 1998, 2010). CRT (1) posits that institutionalized White racism is a structural norm; (2) employs storytelling, where appropriate; and (3) offers a critique of liberalism. It provides a vehicle for the study and reconsideration of race, racism, and power. It facilitates the voice of oppressed peoples—in this case, the voices of Black women principals—and aids in analyzing those all-important voices. It frames the experiences of oppressed peoples, while acknowledging their importance and facilitating their exploration (Crenshaw, Gotada, Peller, & Thomas, 1995). CRT puts into context the truism that some people are privileged while others are not. It acknowledges that while race is a social construct, institutionalized White racism is here to stay. Moreover, it enables us to challenge oppression and privilege through counter-storytelling. In using CRT to frame their studies, many scholars acknowledge race, racism, and power as barriers and challenges for Black women (1) ascending to and navigating within leadership positions and (2) becoming successful in creating schools where all students can succeed. Overall, CRT is an increasingly valuable tool in understanding and hopefully eradicating the social injustice that many Black, brown, red, and yellow children (and other students from oppressed groups) experience in schools every day.

ST focuses on overcoming oppression. It acknowledges that one's position in life impacts his/her ability to acquire knowledge. ST also emphasizes and facilitates storytelling and reflections on personal experiences. When ST is considered in conjunction with BFT—Black Feminist Standpoint Theory (BFST), how individuals view situations and circumstances are linked. BFST is not subscribed to by all Black women; although Black women share many commonalities, they are diverse (e.g., by class, sexual orientation, age, and religious preference). It appears that these two frameworks, BFT and ST, were selected by many scholars whose work is considered herein because of their usefulness in illuminating the life experiences of leaders as well as their leadership practice.

BFT, CRT, and ST are all important frameworks from which to explore the experiences of Black women principals. They each focus on dialogue, or (counter)storytelling. (This may explain, in part, the overreliance in these studies on qualitative research approaches.) They each acknowledge the presence of institutionalized White racism and its impact on oppressed people. CRT sees it as normal, yet calls for its constant reconsideration. ST seeks to eliminate oppression.

BFT is valuable not just because of its focus on institutionalized White racism and because of its spotlight on storytelling. BFT is an African-centered framework that focuses specifically on the Black woman and her unique experiences; it was designed by and for Black women. Moreover, BFT has at its base an acknowledgement of the importance of caring.

### Elementary, Middle, or High School?

There is little discussion in the majority of these studies of the levels of the schools in which the principals served (i.e., elementary, middle, or high school). This is interesting, in part, because in many ways there are differences in leadership and leadership expectations at the three levels. In the area of instructional leadership, for example, elementary school principals interact more in the instructional process than do secondary school principals (Loveless, 2016).

There are implications for principal leadership when we consider the differences in age levels of students in elementary and secondary schools. The interaction with students is not the same at these different levels. Also, there is more interaction between principals and parents at the elementary school level (Child Trends Data Bank, 2013) and more of a focus—or at least a different focus—on discipline at the secondary level (Duncan, 2014).

In four studies, researchers studied principals at all three levels (i.e., elementary, middle, and high school) and considered issues such as commitment to student success (Brown, 2016) and mothering or caring (Carson, 2017). All in all, researchers in 20 studies explored principals at more than one level, seemingly in many cases without consideration for possible differences in leadership practices related to school improvement and parental involvement (Mack, 2010; Roane & Newcomb, 2013, respectively).

When looking at issues related to *the style and context of leading*, consideration of the school level is more important than is the case when looking at issues related to the *lived experiences* of leaders. The distinctions by level are most significant when studying concepts like discipline and instructional leadership—leadership behaviors that vary, depending on the grade level of the students. The distinctions are less significant when looking at the personal attributes and identities of leaders. Comparing the leadership of principals at different levels (as is the case in nearly four out of 10 of these studies) suggests the need to consider the nature of what is being studied first and the significance, if any, of the school level. I now turn to a look at implications for research and principal preparation and professional development.

## Implications

### Research

*Publication avenues.* The large majority of the studies in this review (three out of every four) appear in dissertations. More research is needed in refereed journals and scholarly books. It is not clear why so few studies on Black women principals appear in books and refereed journals. Perhaps the reason lies in the fallacious yet lingering perspective that such work is less legitimate. Generally speaking, the quality of the research—the reliability and validity—is stronger in peer-reviewed journal articles and books published by scholarly presses. If we desire to learn as much as possible about the leadership of Black women principals, we must have more rigorous, high quality research.

*Service levels.* There is an inadequate focus in much of the research on the level of the principal(s)—elementary, middle, or high school. Researchers in a few cases fail to reveal the level at which the principal works or fail to frame their questions in a way that might alert the reader to the unique issues at each level. A greater focus on the level at which the principal is serving would be instructive, given the differences in leadership challenges at the varying levels. More studies differentiating the significance of the school levels for principal leadership are needed. Relatedly, depending upon the focus of the study, it would be useful to compare the leadership of principals at the three levels.

*Methods.* There is a need for more mixed methods studies and more quantitative studies. The focus should be on what Tillman (2002) refers to as culturally sensitive research approaches, wherein the researchers utilize their own (and their subjects') lived experiences, cultural awareness, and expertise to design culturally appropriate research schemes.

There is also a need to place a greater focus on studying schools in addition to interviewing principals largely on their lived experiences. All of the studies included in this review employ qualitative research methods, although a few also include quantitative methods. While the qualitative approaches appear to be more effective with the chosen theoretical frameworks and with the questions being addressed (and given that the focus is on giving voice to these leaders), triangulating the data with quantitative methods, in some cases, may make the findings stronger. More mixed method studies should be conducted. Perhaps some purely quantitative studies would help to shed light on this topic and further efforts to test theories.

As many of the studies considered herein focus on the lived experiences of Black women principals, the focus on qualitative methods—most particularly interviews—is not counterintuitive. As more studies are conducted exploring the *leadership style and context* of Black women principals, increased use of multiple methods and quantitative methods might be expected. Such studies might look, for example, at the impact of the leadership of Black women principals on indicators such as test scores, graduation rates, and suspension rates.

Larger scale studies of student achievement in schools led by Black women principals are needed to shed light on the impact of the leadership of Black women principals. For example, longitudinal studies of graduation rates, suspension rates, post high school choices of graduates, community leadership, etc. would provide benchmarks for preparation programs, as well as for school districts seeking to improve the success of all students.

*Race, racism, and power.* Black women in general, and Black women principals in particular, continue to be oppressed based upon race and gender (and class and age). Some researchers contend that gender has become more significant following the civil rights era (Collins, 2004; Jean-Marie, Williams, & Sherman, 2009; King, 2016; Shorter-Gooden, 2004). The truism regarding these intersecting identities of Black women argues for even more studies looking at this traditionally understudied group of leaders.

Until these and other illegitimate forms of oppression are removed, we all have a responsibility to be social activists. One way that we as academics can do this is with research that further uncovers and ultimately contributes to the eradication of these "isms," especially in light of the studies that illustrate the benefits for students and faculty working under the leadership of Black woman principals.

A few of the studies considered in this review suggest that Black women in the role of principal have to behave differently in order to be successful (e.g., Craig, 2014; Haynes, 2016; Hobson-Horton, 2000; Leathers, 2011; Lewis, 2014; Reed, 2012). This is reminiscent of Du Bois's notion of a double-consciousness, wherein he speaks of an internal conflict experienced by oppressed peoples—the challenge of having two social identities, of being compelled to look at one's self through the eyes of the oppressor. It is a divided identity that one is unable to unify (Du Bois, 1903). This idea is consistent with contemporary research that suggests that Black professional women often find the need to reinvent themselves in the workplace (Durr & Wingfield, 2011). Discrimination based on race (and other illegitimate forms of exclusion) creates challenges for oppressed peoples in general and Black people in particular in attempting to resolve their Americanness and their Blackness. Additional research is needed in this area.

Women leaders are often placed in uniquely challenging and precarious leadership positions in schools and in other leadership settings (Ryan & Haslam, 2005). More studies addressing this issue as it relates to Black women principals would also be useful, assessing the validity of this view and exploring the outcomes of such placements. There is also research that suggests that when women move into leadership roles, particularly women of color, White men tend to become less supportive of the leader (McDonald, Keeves, & Westphal, 2018). It would be instructive to assess the degree to which this behavior is present in schools where Black women serve as the principal and to identify strategies principals and other leaders can use to address this phenomenon.

*Frameworks.* The research explored herein suggests a need to continue the utilization of BFT, CRT, and ST in framing this work. BFT is most appropriate, given its focus on the unique experiences of Black women from an African-centered perspective. CRT aids us in analyzing oppression and the experiences of the oppressed. It is a useful framework for assessing race, racism, and power. As its use is developed within the education arena, it should become even more valuable in analyzing these issues. Finally, ST invites a discussion of oppression and stresses the significance of one's position in life. Moreover, it places an emphasis on the value of lived experiences and storytelling.

Utilizing the above frameworks in concert with relevant leadership theories may be useful. Transformative Leadership Theory, for example, as well as Leadership for Social Justice, are widely promoted as theories that address educational and social inequities, yet both remain relatively untested in authentic contexts (Shields, 2010). Also, Complexity Leadership Theory, which partly focuses on community building, creativity, and adaptability, is consistent with the traits observed in many of the Black women principals in the studies reviewed herein (Uhl-Bien, Marion, & McKelvey, 2007). These and other relevant leadership theories, alone or in combination with CRT, BFT, or ST, might shed new light on how Black women principals' experiences contribute in unique ways to bringing about equitable opportunities for the success of students in their schools.

*Aspects of principal leadership.* I would also call for more studies looking at the leadership strategies of Black women principals. Suggested areas for further consideration might include more studies that look at the significance of communication skills, the level of community engagement, the extent to which goal setting is important, and their role in instructional leadership. There are some studies in most of these areas but far too few. Relatedly, it would be useful to see studies looking at the leadership of Black women principals in comparison to the way that the literature says effective principals lead. That is, of what relevance is that literature on effective principal leadership— derived primarily (up until very recently) from studies of White men principals—to the leadership of Black women principals?

*Urban, suburban, and rural schools.* There are a number of studies looking at Black women principals in urban centers. There are significantly fewer studies looking at Black women principals in suburban and rural communities. As there are differing racial, class, and other factors affecting principal leadership in these environments, studies of Black women principals in these settings would be useful, as would studies comparing the leadership of Black women principals in urban, rural, and suburban schools. Next, I discuss implications for principal preparation and principal professional development.

## Principal Preparation and Principal Professional Development

Among the implications that can be drawn from this review are those related to principal preparation and professional development. For example, the knowledge of the importance of spirituality, or religion, for Black women principals suggests the need to (1) include discussions on spirituality for leaders in school districts and (2) offer content on spirituality and leadership in educational leadership courses.

Mentoring is another type of support these studies identify as significant for the success of Black women principals. The importance of mentoring prospective leaders and new leaders, particularly women, has been widely acknowledged in the research (Adkison, 1981; Allen, Jacobson, & Lomotey, 1995; King, 2012). One area that could be focused on in school districts is stressing the value of—and facilitating—mentoring relationships for Black women principals.

Finally, Black women principals see race and gender as significant issues impacting their leadership efforts. There appear to be several unique sets of circumstances that prevail when Black women are appointed as principals. They include but are not limited to (1) less respect for the position by White men, (2) a more precarious leadership structure, and (3) the principals' experiencing double consciousness. None of this is good and begs to be explored. At a minimum, these issues need to be considered in principal preparation programs and in the professional development of principals. In addition, they should be addressed in teacher preparation programs and professional development for teachers, some of whom (may) work with these leaders.

## Conclusion

I began this article articulating a truism: the persistent, pervasive, and disproportionate disenfranchisement and subsequent underachievement of Black children in U.S. schools. I contend that principals can make a difference, despite the understanding that the teacher/student relationship is paramount. Overall, the literature on Black women principals is, in one sense, too narrowly focused, and I have suggested several ways in which this research can be expanded. More research on these leaders is needed to better understand their potential impact on the success of Black students.

Several strategies currently employed extensively (e.g., CRT and BFT) show promise for additional insightful findings, particularly as researchers intersect them with current and emerging leadership theories. Hopefully, the research will develop in these and other areas and will aid us in addressing the persistent challenges in the principal's office and in the classroom.

Research on Black women principals is a critically important yet relatively new field with far too few published studies. What I have uncovered regarding (1) where this research is published; (2) the thoughts, concerns, and issues of researchers that motivate them to study Black women principals; (3) the theoretical frameworks that are relied upon most often by researchers studying these women; (4) the most popular research methods used by researchers who study these women; (5) the levels at which Black women principals are serving (i.e., elementary, middle, and high school); and (6) the most significant findings from these studies will be important for researchers and practitioners going forward.

In many of the studies reviewed herein, the researchers initially selected as their subjects Black women principals who had reputations as strong, effective leaders. Very often traits such as caring, servant leadership; having some success in combatting racism and sexism; commitment to student success; and community engagement were described. These are stories of unusually courageous and committed women who address inequity and social injustice in their schools every day. This includes efforts toward raising test scores, increasing graduation rates, engaging parents and community members, advancing collaborations, and basically doing whatever is necessary to reduce the opportunity gap for these students to increase the likelihood that all children are successful. The women, in many cases, appeared to understand and personify aspects of culturally responsive leadership. I honor them with this review.

## Notes

1 Much of my own work has focused on the role of Black principals in increasing the success of Black students (Lomotey & Lowery, 2015). I am not suggesting that only Black principals can adequately support Black children. Research suggests that principals, regardless of race, can employ culturally responsive leadership (CRL). There are key components of CRL, and several scholars have observed these components in many principals regardless of race or ethnicity (Horsford, Grosland, & Gunn, 2011; Johnson, 2006; Khalifa, Gooden, & Davis, 2016).

2 While I acknowledge that religion and spirituality are not synonymous, for the purposes of this paper, I use them as such because I believe that the research drawn upon in this review often misuses the term spirituality when referring to religion. That is, while many of the studies cited herein identify a reliance on spirituality by many of these Black women principals, I believe that they are instead relying on their religion, as evidenced by the illustrations that these leaders provide.

3 Bass (2012) explores this notion of caring in what she calls Black Feminist Caring, wherein activism, othermothering, and risk-taking are triggered by the effects of institutionalized White racism and sexism that Black women leaders experience daily.

## References

Abney, E. E. (1980). A comparison of the status of Florida's Black public school principals, 1964–65/1975–76. *Journal of Negro Education, 49*(4), 398–406.

Adkison, J. A. (1981). Women in school administration: A review of the research. *Review of Educational Research, 51*(3), 311–343.

Allen, K., Jacobson, S., & Lomotey, K. (1995). African-American women in educational administration: The importance of mentors and sponsors. *Journal of Negro Education, 64*(4), 409–422.

Armstrong, D., & Mitchell, C. (2017). Shifting identities: Negotiating intersections of race and gender in Canadian administrative contexts. *Educational Management Administration & Leadership, 45*(5), 825–841.

Arnold, N. W., & Brooks, J. S. (2013). Getting churched and being schooled: Making meaning of leadership practice. *Journal of Cases in Educational Leadership, 16*(2), 44–53.

Bagwell, C. L. (2000). *A glimpse into the lives of three African American women principals: A phenomenological approach* (Unpublished doctoral dissertation). Pennsylvania State University, PA.

Bass, L. (2012). When care trumps justice: The operationalization of Black Feminist Caring in educational leadership, *International Journal of Qualitative Studies in Educational Leadership, 25,* 73–87.

Bell, D. A. (1995). Who's afraid of critical race theory? *University of Illinois Law Review, 4,* 893–910.

Best, M. L. (2013). *Assistant principals and reform: A socialization paradox?* (Unpublished doctoral dissertation). University of North Carolina at Chapel Hill, Chapel Hill, NC.

Bloom, C. M., & Erlandson, D. A. (2003). African American women principals in urban schools: Realities, (re)constructions and resolutions. *Education Administration Quarterly, 39*(3), 339–369.

Brown, C. A. (2016). *Understanding the impact of racism and sexism on the development of the professional identity of African American women principals* (Unpublished doctoral dissertation). University of North Carolina at Charlotte, Charlotte, NC.

Carson, D. (2017). *What are the experiences of African American female principals in high-poverty urban schools?* (Doctoral dissertation). Retrieved from ProQuest Dissertations & Theses Global. (Order No. 10753745).

Case, K. I. (1997). African American othermothering in the urban elementary school. *Urban Review, 29*(1), 25–39.

Child Trends Data Bank. (2013). *Parental involvement in schools: Indicators of child and youth-being.* Bethesda, MD: Author.

Collins, P. H. (2004). *Black sexual politics: African Americans, gender, and the new racism.* New York, NY: Routledge.

Craig, L. L. (2014). *Cracks in the ceiling: A case study of African American women principals in a large urban district in the Midwest* (Unpublished doctoral dissertation). Spalding University, Louisville, KY.

Crenshaw, K., Gotada, N., Peller, G., and Thomas, K. (Eds.). (1995). *Critical race theory: The key writings that formed the movement.* New York, NY: The New Press.

Dillard, C. B. (1995). Leading with her life: An African American feminist (re)interpretation of leadership for an urban high school principal. *Educational Administration Quarterly, 31*(4), 539–563.

DuBois, W. E. B. (1903). *The souls of Black folk.* Greenwich, CT: Fawcett.

Duncan, A. (2014). *Rethinking school discipline.* Retrieved from the U.S. Department of Education website: http://www.ed.gov/news/speeches/rethinking-schooldiscipline.

Durr, M., & Wingfield, A. M. H. (2011). Keep your "N" in check: African American women and the interactive effects of etiquette and emotional labor. *Critical Sociology, 37*(5), 557–571.

Eagley, A. H., & Johnson, B. T. (1990). Gender and leadership style: A meta-analysis. *CHIP Documents, 11.* Retrieved from http://digitalcommons.uconn.edu/chip_docs/11.

Fortenberry, D. B. (1987). *A comparison of perceived problems of urban Black and white women principals in elementary, middle, and junior high schools in obtaining the principalship and functioning in that role during their first year* (Unpublished doctoral dissertation). Ball State University, Muncie, IN.

Gillbord, D., & Ladson-Billings, G. (2009). Education and critical race theory. In M. W. Apple, S. J. Ball, & L. A. Gandin (Eds.), *Routledge international handbook of the sociology of education* (pp. 37–47). New York, NY: Routledge.

Haynes, A. M. (2016). *At the intersection of gender and race: A qualitative study of the lived experiences of African American female principals* (Unpublished doctoral dissertation). The University of Nebraska, Omaha, NE.

Heidi, M. (2005). The more things change the more they stay the same: Assessing black underachievement 35 years on. In B. Richardson (Ed.), *Tell it like it is: How our schools fail black children* (pp. 111–119). Stoke-on-Trent, England: Bookmarks and Tretham.

Herndon, J. D. (2002). *Gender differences in high school principals' leadership styles* (Unpublished doctoral dissertation). University of the Pacific, Stockton, CA.

Hobson-Horton, L. (2000). *African American women principals: Examples of urban educational leadership* (Unpublished doctoral dissertation). The University of Wisconsin-Madison, Madison, WI.

Holzman, M. (2012). *A rotting apple: Education redlining in New York City.* Cambridge, MA: The Schott Foundation for Public Education.

hooks, b. (1981). *Ain't I a woman: Black women and feminism.* Troy, NY: South End Press.

Horsford, S. D. (2012). This bridge called my leadership: An essay on Black women as bridge leaders in education. *International Journal of Qualitative Studies in Education, 25*(1), 11–22.

Horsford, S. D., Grosland, T., & Gunn, K. M. (2011). Pedagogy of the personal and professional: Toward a framework for culturally relevant leadership. *Journal of School Leadership, 21*(4), 582–601.

Jean-Marie, G., Williams, V. A., & Sherman, S. L. (2009). Black women's leadership experiences: Examining the intersectionality of race and gender. *Advances in Developing Human Resources, 11*(5), 562–581.

Johnson, L. (2006). "Making her community a better place to live": Culturally responsive urban school leadership in historical context. *Leadership and Policy in Schools, 5*(1), 19–36.

Kelley, G. J. (2012). *How do principals' behaviors facilitate or inhibit the development of a culturally relevant learning community?* (Unpublished doctoral dissertation). Indiana State University, Terre Haute, IN.

Khalifa, M. A., Gooden, M. A., & Davis, J. E. (2016). Culturally responsive school leadership: A synthesis of the literature. *Review of Educational Research, 86*(4), 1272–1311.

King, C. (2012). *The impact of coaching on new African American female principals* (Unpublished doctoral dissertation). California State University, East Bay, Oakland, CA.

King, D. K. (2016). Multiple jeopardy, multiple consciousness: The context of a Black feminist ideology. In B. Landry (Ed.), *Race, Gender and Class: Theory and Methods of Analysis* (pp. 1–23). New York, NY: Routledge.

Kochman, T. (1981). *Black and white styles in conflict.* Chicago, IL: University of Chicago Press.

Ladson-Billings, G. (1998). Just what is critical race theory and what's it doing in a nice field like education? *International Journal of Qualitative Studies in Education, 11*(1), 7–24.

Ladson-Billings, G. (2010). Race. . . to the top, again: Comments on the genealogy of critical race theory. *Connecticut Law Review 43*(5), 1439–1457.

Leathers, S. (2011). *Career path processes as perceived by African American female school principals* (Unpublished doctoral dissertation). University of North Carolina at Chapel Hill, Chapel Hill, NC.

Lee, R. (2007). *How principals promote a culturally relevant learning environment to improve Black student achievement in urban elementary schools* (Unpublished doctoral dissertation). Georgia Southern University, Statesboro, GA.

Lewis, J. R. (2014). *Black females in the principalship: An examination of strategies used to establish and maintain authority* (Unpublished doctoral dissertation). Oakland University, Rochester, MI.

Loder, T. L. (2005). African American women principals' reflections on social change, community, othermothering, and Chicago public school reform. *Urban Education, 40*(3), 298–320.

Lomotey, K. (1989). *African American principals: School leadership and school success.* Westport, CT: Greenwood Press.

Lomotey, K. (1990). *Going to school: The African-American experience.* Albany, NY: State University of New York Press.

Lomotey, K. (1993). African American principals: Bureaucrat/administrators and ethno-humanists. *Urban Education, 27*(4), 395–412.

Lomotey, K., & Lowery, K. (2015). Urban schools, Black principals and Black students: Culturally responsive education and the ethno-humanist role identity. In M. Khalifa, C. Grant, & N. Witherspoon Arnold (Eds.), *Urban school leadership handbook* (pp. 118–134). Lanham, MD: Rowan and Littlefield

Loveless, T. (2016). *The 2016 Brown Center report on American education: How well are American students learning? With sections on reading and math in the common core era, tracking and advanced placement (AP), and principals as instructional leaders.* Washington, DC: The Brown Center on Education Policy at Brookings.

Mack, Y. S. (2010). *Leading school improvement: African American women principals in urban educational settings* (Unpublished doctoral dissertation). University of Cincinnati, Cincinnati, OH.

MacLennan, B. W. (1975). The personalities of group leaders: Implications for selecting and training. *International Journal of Group Psychotherapy, 25*(2), 177–183.

Masci, D. (2018). 5 facts about the religious lives of African Americans. *Pew Research Center.* Retrieved from https://www.sott.net/article/376737-Pew-Research-Five-facts-about-the-religiouslives-of-African-Americans.

Mayienga, D. M. (2013). *Success stories: Biographical narratives of three women school principals in Kenya* (Unpublished doctoral dissertation). Michigan State University, East Lansing, MI.

McDonald, M. L., Keeves, G. D., & Westphal, J. D. (2018). One step forward, one step back: White male top manager organizational identification and helping behavior toward other executives following the appointment of a female or racial minority CEO. *Academy of Management Journal 61*(2), 405–439.

Milner, H. R. (2010). *Start where you are, but don't stay there: Understanding diversity, opportunity gaps, and teaching in today's classrooms.* Cambridge, MA: Harvard Education Press.

Milner, H. R. (2012). Beyond a test score: Explaining opportunity gaps in educational practice. *Journal of Black Studies, 43*(6), 693–718.

Milner, H. R., & Howard, T. C. (2004). Black teachers, black students, black communities, and Brown: Perspectives and insights from experts. *The Journal of Negro Education, 73*(3), 285–297.

Murrell, P. C. (2002). *Developing schools of achievement for African American children.* Albany, NY: State University of New York Press.

National Center for Education Statistics. (2016). *National Teacher and Principal Survey.* Retrieved from https://eric.ed.gov/?id=ED575193.

Page, S. W. (2007). *The courage of our passion: Examining the personal costs negotiated by three African American women executive educational leaders in urban contexts* (Unpublished doctoral dissertation). Texas A&M University, College Station, TX.

Reed, L. C. (2012). The intersection of race and gender in school leadership for three Black female principals. *International Journal of Qualitative Studies in Education, 25*(1), 39–58.

Reitzug. U. C., & Patterson, J. (1998). "I'm not going to lose you!" Empowerment through caring in an urban principal's practice with students. *Urban Education, 33*(2), 150–181.

Roane, T., & Newcomb, W. (2013). Experiences of young African American women principals. *Leading and Managing, 19*(1), 1–17.

Rogers, E. M., & Shoemaker, F. F. (1971). *Communication of innovation: A cross-cultural approach.* New York, NY: Free Press.

Ryan, M. K., & Haslam, S. A. (2005). The glass cliff: Evidence that women are over-represented in precarious leadership positions. *British Journal of Management, 16*(2), 81–90.

Shields, C. M. (2010). Transformative leadership: Working for equity in diverse contexts. *Educational Administration Quarterly, 46*(4). 558–589.

Shorter-Gooden, K. (2004). Multiple resistance strategies: How African American women cope with racism and sexism. *Journal of Black Psychology, 30*(3), 406–425.

Shujaa, M. J., & Shujaa, K. J. (Eds.). (2015). *The SAGE encyclopedia of African cultural heritage in North America.* Thousand Oaks, CA: SAGE.

Spicer, Y. M. (2004). *"Our experience says we know something: We are still here". An autoethnographic study of African American women principals in Massachusetts K-12 public schools* (Unpublished doctoral dissertation). University of Massachusetts-Boston, Boston, MA.

Tillman, L. C. (2002). Culturally sensitive research approaches: An African-American perspective. *Educational Researcher, 31*(9), 3–12.

Tillman, L. (2004). African American principals and the legacy of Brown. *Review of Research in Education, 28*(1), 101–146.

Turner, C. T. (2004). *Voices of four African American and European American female principals and their leadership styles in a recognized urban school district* (Unpublished doctoral dissertation). Texas A&M University, College Station, TX.

Tweedle, P. W. D. (1996). *A study of the career paths of African-American women principals in the elementary schools of Chicago, Illinois, appointed before and after the implementation of school reform* (Unpublished doctoral dissertation). University of Illinois at Urbana-Champaign, Urbana-Champaign, IL.

Uhl-Bien, M., Marion, R., & McKelvey, B. (2007). Complexity leadership theory: Shifting leadership from the industrial age to the knowledge era. *The Leadership Quarterly, 18*(4), 298–318.

Williams, I., & Loeb, S. (2012). *Race and the principal pipeline: The prevalence of minority principals in light of a largely white teacher workforce.* Stanford, CA: Center for Education Policy Analysis.

## Appendix A

### Bibliography of Studies on Black Women Principals Included in This Review

Acheampong, L. (2009). *An inquiry into the leadership experiences of African American women principals in Catholic schools* (Unpublished doctoral dissertation). Fordham University, New York, NY.

Aldaco, A. L. G. (2016). *Fiery passion and relentless commitment: The lived experiences of African American women principals in turnaround model schools* (Unpublished doctoral dissertation). Texas State University, San Marcos, TX.

Bagwell, C. L. (2000). *A glimpse into the lives of three African American women principals: A phenomenological approach* (Unpublished doctoral dissertation). Pennsylvania State University, State College, PA.

Beckford-Bennett, K. V. (2009). *Visible now: The challenges faced by Black female principals leading in predominantly White school settings* (Unpublished doctoral dissertation). University of Pennsylvania, Philadelphia, PA.

Berry, S. D. (2008). *Principals of critical spirituality: African American females in elementary urban schools* (Unpublished doctoral dissertation). Texas A&M University, College Station, TX.

Bloom, C. M. (2001). *Critical race theory and the African American woman principal: Alternative portrayals of effective leadership practice in urban schools* (Unpublished doctoral dissertation). Texas A&M University, College Station, TX.

Bloom, C. M., & Erlandson, D. A. (2003). African American women principals in urban schools: Realities, (re)constructions, and resolutions. *Educational Administration Quarterly, 39*(3), 339–369.

Brown, C. A. (2016). *Understanding the impact of racism and sexism on the development of the professional identity of African American women principals* (Unpublished doctoral dissertation). University of North Carolina at Charlotte, Charlotte, NC.

Brown, T. M. M. (2009). *The perceptions of African American women principals who have been influential in public education* (Unpublished doctoral dissertation). Robert Morris University, Moon, PA.

Byrd, C., Sr. (2009). *Voices of identity and responsibility: A description of the development of identity using Cross' theory of Nigrescence* (Unpublished doctoral dissertation). Cardinal Stritch University, Milwaukee, WI.

Cain, J. A. (2016). *Understanding the experiences and perceptions of the African American female principal* (Unpublished doctoral dissertation). Saint Louis University, St. Louis, MO.

Carson, D. (2017). *What are the experiences of African American female principals in high-poverty urban schools?* (Doctoral dissertation). Retrieved from ProQuest Dissertations & Theses Global. (Order No. 10753745)

Carter, S. A. (2013). *The influences of race and gender on the leadership of African American female principals in predominantly white elementary schools* (Unpublished doctoral dissertation). Seton Hall University, South Orange, NJ.

Case, K. I. (1997). African American othermothering in the urban elementary school. *Urban Review, 29*(1), 25–39.

Collins, V. P. (2015). *Listening to the voices of African American female principals leading "turnaround" schools* (Unpublished doctoral dissertation). University of Denver, Denver, CO.

Cox, B. (2013). *"A Song for You" as tribute to the daughters of the South: Illuminating the work of Black women principals* (Unpublished doctoral dissertation). Georgia Southern University, GA.

Craig, L. L. (2014). *Cracks in the ceiling: A case study of African American women principals in a large urban district in the Midwest* (Unpublished doctoral dissertation). Spalding University, Louisville, KY.

Dillard, C. B. (1995). Leading with her life: An African American feminist (re)interpretation of leadership for an urban high school principal. *Educational Administration Quarterly, 31*(4), 539–563.

Gray, P. L. (2014). *Contemporary othermothering and the principalship: How gender and culture impact the identities of African American female secondary principals* (Doctoral dissertation). Retrieved from ProQuest Dissertations & Theses Global. (Order No. 3637079)

Griffin, S. V. (2007). *The satisfaction and dissatisfaction of African American women administrators using transformational leadership practices* (Unpublished doctoral dissertation). Fielding Graduate University, Santa Barbara, CA.

Haynes, A. M. (2016). *At the intersection of gender and race: A qualitative study of the lived experiences of African American female principals* (Unpublished doctoral dissertation). The University of Nebraska, Omaha, NE.

Hobson-Horton, L. (2000). *African American women principals: Examples of urban educational leadership* (Unpublished doctoral dissertation). University of Wisconsin-Madison, Madison, WI.

Hooper, A. B. (2002). *The role of spirituality in the work of African-American women principals in urban schools* (Unpublished doctoral dissertation). The University of Wisconsin-Madison, Madison, WI.

Ingram, B. C. (2016). *After opportunity knocks: Factors associated with the persistence of middle- and late-career African American female principals* (Unpublished doctoral dissertation). Ashland University, Ashland, OH.

Jackson, A. D. (2013). *Fighting through resistance: Challenges faced by African American women principals in predominately White school settings* (Unpublished doctoral dissertation). Capella University.

Jean-Marie, G. (2013). The subtlety of age, gender, and race barriers: A case study of early career African American female principals. *Journal of School Leadership, 23*(4), 615.

Johnson, J. M. (2017). *Wonder women: Partially visible, fully indispensable: A multi-case study of the perspectives of African American women school leaders on leadership, influence and power* (Unpublished doctoral dissertation). University of Pennsylvania, Philadelphia, PA.

Johnson, L. (2006). "Making her community a better place to live": Culturally responsive urban school leadership in historical context. *Leadership and Policy in Schools, 5*(1), 19–36.

King, C. (2012). *The impact of coaching on new African American female* (Unpublished doctoral dissertation). California State University, East Bay, Oakland, CA.

Leathers, S. (2011). *Career path processes as perceived by African American female school principals* (Unpublished doctoral dissertation). University of North Carolina at Chapel Hill, Chapel Hill, NC.

Lee, R. (2007). *How principals promote a culturally relevant learning environment to improve Black student achievement in urban elementary schools* (Unpublished doctoral dissertation). Georgia Southern University, Statesboro, GA.

Lewis, J. R. (2014). *Black females in the principalship: An examination of strategies used to establish and maintain authority* (Unpublished doctoral dissertation). Oakland University, Rochester, MI.

Loder, T. L. (2005). African American women principals' reflections on social change, community othermothering, and Chicago public school reform. *Urban Education, 40*(3), 298–320.

Lomotey, K. (1993). African American principals: Bureaucrat/administrators and ethno-humanists. *Urban Education, 27*(4), 395–412.

Mack, Y. S. (2010). *Leading school improvement: African American women principals in urban educational settings* (Unpublished doctoral dissertation). University of Cincinnati, Cincinnati, OH.

McArthur, A. M. (2009). *Reflections on leadership: Exploring the perspectives of Black women secondary school principals* (Unpublished doctoral dissertation). Teachers College, Columbia University, New York, NY.

Miles Brown, T. M. (2009). *The perceptions of African American women principals who have been influential in public education* (Unpublished doctoral dissertation). Robert Morris University, Moon, PA.

Newcomb, W. S., & Khan, I. L. (2014). Embracing spirituality: African American women leaders pushing the evolution of leadership practices in schools. In N. W. Arnold, M. Brooks, & B. M. Arnold (Eds.), *Critical perspectives on Black education: Spirituality, religion and social justice* (pp. 1–29). Charlotte, NC: Information Age Publishing.

Newcomb, W. S., & Niemeyer, A. (2015). African American women principals: Heeding the call to serve as conduits for transforming urban school communities. *International Journal of Qualitative Studies in Education, 28*(7), 786–799.

Peters, A. L. (2003). *A case study of an African American female principal participating in an administrative leadership academy* (Unpublished doctoral dissertation). Ohio State University, Columbus, OH.

Peters, A. L. (2012). Leading through the challenge of change: African-American women principals on small school reform. International *Journal of Qualitative Studies in Education, 25*(1), 23–38.

Prescott-Hutchins, S. R. (2002). *The challenges and successes of African American women principals in Georgia: A qualitative profile of lived experiences* (Unpublished doctoral dissertation). Georgia Southern University, Statesboro, GA.

RESEARCH ON THE LEADERSHIP OF BLACK WOMEN PRINCIPALS 89

Reed, L. C. (2012). The intersection of race and gender in school leadership for three Black female principals. *International Journal of Qualitative Studies in Education, 25*(1), 39–58.

Reed, L., & Evans, A. (2008). "What you see is [not always] what you get!" Dispelling race and gender leadership assumptions. *International Journal of Qualitative Studies in Education, 21*(5), 487–49.

Reitzug, U. C., & Patterson, J. (1998). "I'm not going to lose you!" Empowerment through caring in an urban principal's practice with students. *Urban Education, 33*(2), 150–181.

Renix, A. D. (2016). *Declaring the truth of her voice: Portraits of African American women principals and the staff cultures they lead* (Unpublished doctoral dissertation). Howard University, Washington, DC.

Roane, T., & Newcomb, W. (2013). Experiences of young African American women principals. *Leading and Managing, 19*(1), 1–17.

Rogers, E. M., & Shoemaker, F. F. (1971). *Communication of innovation: A cross-cultural approach.* New York, NY: Free Press.

Rose, S. A. (2013). *An autoethnographic study: An African American woman's perception of her journey to the principalship* (Unpublished doctoral dissertation). Texas A&M University, College Station, TX.

Ross, S. D. F. (2001). *African American women principals: The East Texas experience* (Unpublished doctoral dissertation). Stephen F. Austin State University, Nacogdoches, TX.

Smith, S. I. (2009). *Exploring leadership through spiritual practices and African moral virtues: Portraits of African American women principals in urban settings* (Unpublished doctoral dissertation). Indiana University, Bloomington, IN.

Spicer, Y. M. (2004). *"Our experience says we know something: We are still here." An autoethnographic study of African American women principals in Massachusetts K-12 public schools* (Unpublished doctoral dissertation), University of Massachusetts-Boston, Boston, MA.

Taylor, C. R. (2004). *An inquiry into the experiences of the African American woman principal: Critical race theory and the Black feminist perspectives* (Unpublished doctoral dissertation). Georgia Southern University, Statesboro, GA.

Taylor, L. (2014). *A multiple case study of two African American female administrators in high achieving elementary schools* (Unpublished doctoral dissertation). University of North Texas, Denton, TX.

Tweedle, P. W. D. (1996). *A study of the career paths of African-American women principals in the elementary schools of Chicago, Illinois, appointed before and after the implementation of school reform* (Unpublished doctoral dissertation). University of Illinois at Urbana-Champaign, Champaign, IL.

Wallis, T. V. (2016). *21st century transformational leadership: The neostereotypical phenomenon of a Black female principal* (Unpublished doctoral dissertation). Louisiana State University, Baton Rouge, LA.

Wells, C. (2013). *The balance of two worlds: A study of the perceptions of African American female principals and leadership* (Unpublished doctoral dissertation). Texas A&M University-Kingsville, Kingsville, TX.

Williams, C. (2013). *Women's leadership: A study of African American female principal experiences* (Unpublished doctoral dissertation). The Florida State University, Tallahassee, FL.

## Appendix B

### Age Range of Black Women Principals in U.S. Public Schools: 2015–2016

| Age Range | Number | Percentage |
| --- | --- | --- |
| <45 | 2,500 | 39 |
| 45–55 | 2,430 | 38 |
| >55 | 1,400 | 22 |

## Appendix C

### Black Women Principal Tenure in U.S. Public Schools: 2015–2016

| Tenure as Principal | Number | Percentage |
| --- | --- | --- |
| <2 years | 1,250 | 20 |
| 2–3 years | 1,380 | 22 |
| 4–9 years | 2,210 | 35 |
| 10 years + | 1,510 | 24 |

## Appendix D

### Academic Preparation of Black Women Principals in U.S. Public Schools: 2015–2016

| Degree | Number | Percentage |
|---|---|---|
| Bachelor of arts | 140 | 2 |
| Master's | 2,850 | 45 |
| Ed specialist | 2,060 | 32 |
| Doctorate | 1,290 | 20 |

## Appendix E

### Number of Studies of Black Women Principals by Year

| Publication Year | # of Studies Published |
|---|---|
| 1993–1996 | 2 |
| 1997–2000 | 5 |
| 2001–2004 | 8 |
| 2005–2008 | 6 |
| 2009–2012 | 12 |
| 2013–2017 | 24 |
| Total | 57 |

## Appendix F

### Methodological Tools Used

| Tool | # of Studies |
|---|---|
| Interviews | 44 |
| Observations | 12 |
| Document review | 5 |
| Narrative inquiry | 4 |
| Survey | 3 |
| Focus groups | 3 |
| Case studies | 3 |
| Autoethnographies | 2 |
| Artifacts | 2 |
| Other | 5 |

## Appendix G
### Level of Schools in Which Principals Served

| School Level(s) | # of Studies |
|---|---|
| Combination | 27 |
| Elementary schools | 15 |
| High schools | 10 |
| Information not provided | 4 |
| Middle schools | 1 |
| Total | 57 |

## Appendix H
### What Black, White, and Latino/a People Say About Their Religiosity

| Group | They Believe in God With Absolute Certainty | Religion Is Very Important | They Pray Daily | They Attend Religious Services at Least Weekly |
|---|---|---|---|---|
| Blacks | 83 | 75 | 73 | 47 |
| Whites | 59 | 59 | 58 | 39 |
| Latino/a | 61 | 49 | 52 | 34 |

*Source.* Adapted from U.S. Religious Landscape Study (2014), cited in Masci (2018).

## *Afterthought*

It would be interesting to do a follow-up review of the leadership of Black women principals, given the growth in the number of studies over the years. As shown in Appendix E of this 2019 study, I placed the studies in 4-year clusters (1993–1996, 1997–2000, etc.). The clusters show a near-constant increase in the number of studies; in all but one cluster, the number of studies increased significantly. In the first grouping (1993–1996) there were only two studies. By 2013–2017 there were 24 studies. The next grouping would be 2018–2021, and I suspect the number would exceed 24, buttressing the argument for a follow-up study.

## *Discussion Questions*

1. Compare and contrast the role and significance of the teacher and the principal in bringing about academic, social, cultural, and spiritual success of Black students.

2. Why do you believe there are now approximately twice as many Black female principals as there are Black male principals (particularly given the overwhelming preponderance of Black males in these positions pre-*Brown*)?

3. Consider the significance of the findings from this literature review for the education of Black students.

## *References*

Dunbar, J. N. (2015). *African-American males, African-American female principals, and the opportunity gap* [Unpublished doctoral dissertation]. Georgia Southern University.

Lomotey, K. (2019). Research on the leadership of Black women principals: Implications for Black students. *Educational Researcher, 48*(9), 336–348.

Tillman, L. C. (2004). African American principals and the legacy of Brown. *Review of Research in Education, 28,* 101–146.

U.S. Equal Employment Opportunity Commission. (2018). *Job patterns for minorities and women in elementary-secondary public schools (EEO-5).* https://www.eeoc.gov/statistics/job-patterns-minorities-and-women-elementary-secondary-public-schools-eeo-5

5.

# THE LEADERSHIP OF BLACK MALE PRINCIPALS: WHAT THE RESEARCH TELLS US

The major focus of this book is my concern for the academic and overall success of Black children in U.S. schools and in society generally. I am concerned about the academic, social, cultural, and spiritual success of these children. The masses of these youth have not done well in U.S. schools (and society) since African people initially arrived on these shores more than 500 years ago (Lomotey, 1990). This book addresses the role of educational institutions in improving the overall success of Black children. More particularly, I seek to articulate the role of Black male and female principals in the success of Black children.

There is some evidence that there are gender differences in leadership styles. In this chapter, I look at the research that has been done on the leadership of Black male principals, in particular. (In Chapter 4, I reprinted my 2019 *Educational Researcher* article focusing on the leadership of Black women principals.) Given that most of the authors whose work is reviewed in this chapter employ Critical Race Theory (CRT) as a theoretical frame for their examinations, in this chapter, I also describe CRT.

## *Background*

Black principals, like Black teachers, play an important role in the overall success of Black students. There is significance in the cultural connection between Black students and Black principals.

That is, their shared values, background, beliefs, and so on tend to lead to more meaningful and effective communication, ultimately contributing to greater student success. It is this truism that has led me to focus much of my research on Black principals over the past 40 or more years. This tendency toward higher overall success for Black students also comes about because Black educators tend to have higher expectations for Black students.

Prior to the *Brown v. Board of Education* case, Black male principals were the norm within Black schools in the U.S. while, in these schools, women were the overwhelmingly predominant group within the teaching force. According to Tillman (2004),

> Consistent with the time period, most of the pre-*Brown* principals were men. While the contributions of Black female principals are acknowledged in the research, it was expected that the principal would be male and that he would be accorded recognition and respect based on his gender. These expectations suggest that Black women who aspired to the principalship faced a sexist environment. However, the post-*Brown* period would see a gradual shift in the demographics of the principalship, as more Black women would lead schools (particularly at the elementary level) two decades after the *Brown* decision. (p.14)

Despite the overwhelming predominance of Black men as principals pre-*Brown*, as Tillman suggests, we have numerous accounts of Black women courageously leading educational institutions during this period. Further evidence of the presence of Black women school leaders is provided by Dunbar (2015), who cites the school leadership of several prominent Black women, including Sarah Smith, Mary McLeod Bethune, and Fannie Jackson Coppin, who were social activists and role models for aspiring Black women school leaders.

More recently, the numbers—as they relate to the Black principalship—have shifted in favor of Black women. Black women

# THE LEADERSHIP OF BLACK MALE PRINCIPALS

outnumber Black men nearly two to one in the principalship in U.S. public schools (U.S. Equal Employment Opportunity Commission, 2018). This is true, in part, because of the excessively high turnover rate for Black male teachers. Principals overwhelmingly come from the teaching ranks. If a significant number of Black male teachers are leaving the teaching ranks, this will contribute to a subsequent reduction in their numbers in administrative positions.

An obvious question springing up from this truism is: What are the implications of this massive shift—from a cadre of overwhelmingly Black male principals to significantly more Black woman principals—for Black children? Generally, I would say that the jury is still out regarding the significance of this shift. The truth is that there is too little data in this area; that is, there is insufficient research that explores the significance of Black principals—male or female—for the success of Black students in U.S. schools. However, despite this plethora of research, it appears as though—to date—there has been no notable impact on the overall success of Black children resulting from this change.

We do know some things about the leadership of Black women principals that may be cause for optimism—and an impetus for additional research. We know, for example, that Black women principals do tend to display a beneficial mothering behavior with Black children. This is reflected in the literature on these leaders with encouraging terms like othermothering, passion, and caring.

## *Methods*

In this chapter, I review the research on Black male principals during the period 1975–2021. This range in years is somewhat misleading. The overwhelming majority of the studies reviewed herein (27 of 29) were published between 2007 and 2021. Only two studies are from before that period: Banks (1975) and Turbyfill (1997).

I examine dissertations, journal articles, book chapters, and a book. The exploration was done through Western Carolina

University's (WCU's) Hunter Library. Assistance was provided by Beth McDonough, a (now retired) Research and Instruction Librarian. Additional support was provided by two WCU graduate assistants, Tyler Oreskovic and Bryan Stewart. I review 29 studies that appear primarily in dissertations.

## Research Questions

1.  What do we know about the leadership of Black male principals?
2.  What types of research (e.g., methodologies, frameworks, and publication types) are focused on Black male principals?
3.  What is the nature of the explorations that focus on Black male principals?

## *Findings*

### What types of research (e. g., methodologies, types of publications) are done on Black male principals?

I uncovered 29 published research studies that focus specifically on Black male principals (see Appendix). As is the case with most research on educational leadership, most of the research on Black male principals was published in dissertations (24, or 83%; Bridges, 1982 Lomotey, 2019). Additional studies were printed in journal articles (3, or 10%), an Education Resources Information Center (ERIC) publication, and a book.

The plurality of these publications were published in 2014 (5) and in 2018 (5). An average of nearly three were published each year between 2014 and 2021. Prior to that, the average number of publications beginning in 2006 was one per year.

Six of the 29 studies (21%) are of Black male elementary school principals. Three (10%) focus on high school principals, and one (3%) is a study of middle school principals. Nineteen studies (66%) include principals from a mixture of levels (i.e., elementary, middle, and high school).

THE LEADERSHIP OF BLACK MALE PRINCIPALS 99

All 29 studies are qualitative with some combination of interviews, focus groups, observations, and document review. The sample sizes of these studies range from 1 to 14, with a single mode of five.

The authors of 16 of the 29 studies (55%) employ CRT to provide a theoretical frame for their inquiries. In part, because of the heavy reliance upon CRT, I provide a description of this theoretical framework for the reader.

*Critical Race Theory.* Law scholars with major responsibility for the initial articulation of CRT include Derrick Bell (1995), his protégé, Kimberle Crenshaw (Crenshaw et al., 1995), and Richard Delgado (Delgado & Stefanic, 2012), among others. Initially, CRT provided a vehicle through which legal scholars could ascertain how racial disparities are reinforced in courts. Through CRT, we also begin to understand how racism remains—despite the removal, in some cases, of the policies that brought it about.

While it is common knowledge that critical race theory had its origins in the field of law, since the 1980's, countless academics have employed and built upon those initial conceptions of critical race theory in order to better comprehend the sizable and noteworthy impact of race on every aspect of society—from health to politics to education. These academics contend that CRT has been around since the 1980s, and has been used widely, by them and myriad other academics. Further, they argue that it is a legitimate framework used to fathom the impact of race and racism in U.S. society.

With CRT, scholars argue for the destruction of vehicles that reinforce institutionalized White supremacy. They call for a dismantling of racist structures within this society and, particularly, a demolition of policies that work to maintain the status quo—wherein a few remain in power, and many continue to be oppressed and powerless. In utilizing CRT, academics in law initially—and, later, other scholars—researched how social injustice is perpetuated by legal structures. Importantly, CRT necessitates bringing to the forefront the voices of the oppressed—*those who suffer the most* because of racism and widespread racial disparities. Here I emphasize those who suffer the most, while acknowledging that we all suffer because of institutionalized White supremacy.

CRT represents a vehicle through which scholars throughout academia (including those whose works are highlighted in this chapter) look at racism and racial disparities and their impact on the oppressed and the powerless to discover, from their disciplinary lens, how such gross differences are perpetuated.

The movement of CRT into the field of education was facilitated initially by Gloria Ladson-Billings and William Tate in 1995 (Ladson-Billings & Tate, 1995). In education, be it pre-K–12, community college, or 4-year college/university, CRT is a tool that we use to analyze, disrupt, and transform educational institutions to bring about equitable and socially just outcomes for students, their families, and the communities in which they live. With schooling, CRT is utilized to explore the relationship between educational policy and inequalities. CRT assumes the inherent value of a culturally responsive educational experience for all students. It utilizes the voice of those who suffer the most because of institutionalized White supremacy (Lomotey, 2019).

CRT facilitates the examination of the role and impact of race and racism in legal, educational, and social disciplines. It offers a theoretical context that calls attention to—and enables us to examine—the existence of race and racism and how race and racism play a role in the social fabric of the U.S. (Crenshaw et al., 1995; Parker & Lynn, 2002). Using CRT, scholars rely on the viewpoints, experiences, and expertise of Black, Latinx, and Indigenous Peoples—people who suffer the most because of racial disparities.

We explore the reality of these groups with CRT. The theory presumes that institutionalized White supremacy exists and that it permeates our society. According to CRT, institutionalized White supremacy encompasses more than one's personal prejudice. It is ingrained in legal structures, policies, and institutions. CRT enables us to analyze the oppression and overall experiences of the oppressed. It provides a lens to assess the so-called realities foisted upon Black, Latinx, and Indigenous Peoples by those who are in power. Of course, people in power define reality and convince others that it is *their* reality.

CRT is based on five prominent tenets: (a) counter-storytelling; (b) the permanence of institutionalized White supremacy; (c) Whiteness as property; (d) interest convergence; and (e) the critique of liberalism. Counter-storytelling occurs when Black, Latinx, and Indigenous Peoples share their experiences and knowledge, correcting the racialized ideologies created *about* them—by others. It is also an approach my colleagues in academia use to co-construct the experiences of those whose voices have been marginalized or silenced by the narratives of those in power. Interest convergence holds that White elites will tolerate or encourage racial advances for Blacks and other marginalized groups *only* when such advances promote White self-interest.

CRT is not a racist, distorted, biased re-writing of history or of reality. In fact, CRT is an honest assessment and critique of the racist power structure in the U.S. and an effort to expose and eradicate institutionalized White supremacy. In the studies reviewed herein and in tens of thousands of studies in education and other disciplines, CRT provides an honest framing of the experiences of marginalized folk. It highlights the importance of their experiences and the exploration thereof. *The overall goal of CRT is to eradicate social injustice, inequity, and oppression experienced by Black, Latinx, Indigenous Peoples, and all marginalized peoples brought about because of institutionalized White supremacy* (Lomotey, in press).

Other theories employed by the researchers whose works I have reviewed for this chapter include Leader–Member Exchange, African American Male, Transformative Leadership, Resilience, Adult Development, Self-Efficacy, Black Masculine Caring, and Human Motivational Needs.

## What is the nature of the explorations that focus upon Black male principals?

*Lived Experiences/Challenges.* Ten of the 29 studies (34%) address aspects of the lived experiences (and associated challenges) faced by Black male principals (Adkins-Sharif, 2020; Brooks, 2017; Carter-Oliver, 2014; Funchess, 2014; Grubbs, 2021; Moultry, 2014; J. Smith, 2019; P. A. Smith, 2019, 2021; Thomas, 2018).

Adkins-Sharif (2020), in a dissertation, conducted an ethnography of three Black male principals. Using CRT, he performed interviews and a focus group, exploring the degree to which these leaders focused on social justice aimed at countering racism, institutionalized White supremacy, anti-Blackness, racial disparities, and White privilege. He ascertained that these leaders were centered in the concept of race, believed in racial power, and saw their role as conducting healing and empowering work.

In a dissertation, Brooks (2017) looks at the post-Brown experiences of Black male principals. Utilizing CRT to examine five elementary school principals, she uncovered six themes highlighted by servant leadership and positive relationships with Black male students.

Carter-Oliver (2014) used CRT to explore the experiences of five Black male principals in St. Louis during the 20-year period from 1960 to 1980. The results indicate that these principals focused on personnel decisions, central office communication, student discipline, and improving student achievement. Interestingly, the first two foci reflect the bureaucrat/administrator role identity, while the latter two are consistent with ethno-humanism.

Funchess (2014) conducted interviews of four Black male principals, exploring the impact of their experiences and values on their decision-making. In this dissertation, evidence indicates that spirituality was important to these men in their leadership, as was integrity and providing an example for their students. They cared for their students and for the communities from which they came. Collaboration and collectivism were important to these leaders. In

# THE LEADERSHIP OF BLACK MALE PRINCIPALS 103

Chapter 4, I cite an overwhelming emphasis on the importance of spirituality by Black women principals. I find it interesting that in only two of the 29 studies uncovered for this review was spiritualism noted as being of significance for these male principals (Funchess, 2014; Johnson, 2018).

In a 2021 dissertation, Grubbs focused on the challenges, barriers, and support mechanisms experienced by five Black male principals. Using interviews, observations, and document analysis, he determined several things; most notably, these individuals were instructional leaders, they were mentors, and they were innovative. In addition, these Black male principals experienced macroaggressions, had challenges leading White staff, and often found it necessary to code-switch.

In another dissertation, Moultry (2014) explores the lived experiences of four Black male elementary school principals. Using CRT, he notes that: (1) many ways of learning were employed by the principals, (2) they each had different experiences in their upbringing, (3) they had mentors and networks, (4) they valued high-quality teachers, and (5) they embodied caring personalities.

J. Smith (2019) carried out a study of six Black male principals, providing narratives of their experiences serving in predominantly White schools. Using CRT and qualitative methods in this dissertation, he notes: (1) the importance of family connections, (2) the significance of power in seeking to redress injustices, (3) the value of inclusive communities, and (4) that they were perceived as a threat to Whiteness.

Thomas (2018) also looked at the experiences of Black male principals in predominantly White schools. The emerging themes illustrate the importance of support and motivation and the significance of navigating White spaces. Thomas employed CRT in this qualitative study.

P.A. Smith (2019, 2021) studied the significance of identities and other experiences for the leadership of Black male principals. He highlights social justice advocacy, civil rights activism, and addressing inequities and strategies used by these leaders.

*Career Aspirations.* In 6 of the 29 studies (21%), the researchers address issues related to the career aspirations of *prospective* Black male principals and *sitting* Black male principals (Banks, 1975; Black, 2012; Humphrey, 2007; Jackson, 2018; Johnson, 2018; Miller, 2008).

Banks (1975) conducted qualitative case studies of five successful Black male elementary school principals. Using CRT, he studied the experiences of these principals. His exploration addresses obstacles experienced by these leaders en route to their principalships, as well as other experiences of these successful principals. Banks's findings highlight the importance of several factors, most notably, transformational leadership and the support of Black role models.

Black (2012) also published an article exploring the various barriers and obstacles encountered by Black males in pursuing principalships. The author ascertained that, among other things, Black male principals: (1) display transformational leadership, (2) focus on learning from individuals around them, (3) serve as role models for others, and (4) continue to encounter barriers.

Humphrey's 2017 dissertation offers an exploration of the career trajectory of 12 Black male high school principals. Extracting from semi-structured interviews, he discovered that these leaders: (1) had significant support groups, (2) had a goal early on of becoming a principal, (3) were confident, and (4) had important mentors and encouragement from other colleagues.

Jackson (2018) explored the recruitment process and other factors associated with the teacher-to-principal pipeline. He discovered that: (1) no specific efforts were made to recruit Black male principals, though applicants were not dissuaded from applying; (2) confidence was critically important; (3) there should be targeted recruitment efforts; (4) there are too few Black male principals; and (5) better retention efforts are needed once these leaders are appointed.

In another dissertation, using Resiliency Theory, Johnson (2018) examined the resiliency of 10 Black male school leaders as they pursued their principalships. The findings indicate the importance of: (1) networking and mentoring, (2) family and church, (3) faith, (4) ethics, (5) persistence, and (6) the significance of overcoming challenges.

Miller (2008) looked at the career paths of five Black male elementary school principals, using Adult Development Theory as a frame. The principals noted their (1) persona and professional fulfillment, and (2) various significant challenges, as well as (3) the rapidly declining number of Black male principals.

*Commitment to Students.* There are six (21%) studies in which the researchers address issues associated with the relationship between the Black male principal and Black students. More particularly, these scholars look at the impact of these relationships on student success (Brooks, 2017; Dawson, 2018; Derrick, 2009; Miller, 2019; Palija, 2020; Washington, 2019).

In a 2017 dissertation, Brooks conducted case studies of five Black male elementary school principals—focusing on their lived experiences. (The reader will, no doubt, note some overlap here. Several studies fall into more than one category. For example, Brooks [2017] falls within the Lived Experiences category as well as the Commitment to Students category.)

The explorations concentrate on these principals' post-*Brown* experiences and their commitment to Black students. Using CRT, Brooks uncovers six themes. Highlights of the findings include these principals focusing on servant leadership and relationships with Black students.

In a dissertation, Dawson (2018) looks at the leadership styles of Black male principals and particularly at the relationship between eight such leaders and Black male students. Utilizing CRT as a framework, she conducted a qualitative study. Her results show that the principals in the study supported Black male students by: (1) encouraging positive relationships, (2) promoting support, and (3) noting exclusionary disciplinary practices.

In a 2009 dissertation, Derrick reports on interviews of two Black male high school principals, highlighting their impact on Black male students. Of note, race was not focused on in the interviews and was not uncovered as a significant factor. The mentoring of these students did appear to have a positive effect for the students.

Miller (2019) looks at factors affecting the leadership of Black male principals and how Black students benefit from the presence of a Black principal. Using CRT in this case study of 10 principals, he highlights the importance of Black male principals mentoring and building relationships with Black students to bring about their success. The significance of the ethno-humanist role identity is highlighted by Miller; he uses the components thereof to describe the leadership qualities of the subjects.

Palija (2020), using CRT in a qualitative study, explores the impact of three Black male principals on Black male students. The findings indicate that these leaders: (1) had strong Black males in their lives, (2) emphasized professional development in their schools, and (3) valued a diverse and culturally competent faculty.

Washington (2019) looks at the relationships between two Black male principals and the Black male students in their all-male elementary schools. In this dissertation, he notes the importance of: (1) relationships with students, (2) cultural connections, and (3) school reform.

*Principal Characteristics.* In terms of focus, 5 of the 29 studies (17%) address the characteristics of Black male principals (Anderson, 2015; Henderson, 2015; Rivera-McCutchen, 2021; J. Smith, 2019; Turbyfill, 1997). In a book exploring staff perceptions of the leadership of Black male principals, Anderson (2015) utilizes Leader–Member Exchange Theory. Specifically, he explores: (1) staff views of the leaders' images, (2) relations with staff, and (3) leadership qualities. He concludes that positive staff relationships are important, as is effective leadership focused on pursuing the institution's vision.

Henderson, in a journal article (2015), explores the values, beliefs, and leadership practices of six Black male high school principals. He uses a survey, interviews, and a focus group in this qualitative study. He discovered that these leaders moved beyond the school to address larger social and systemic issues that impacted the success of their students. They employed an integrated leadership style to be effective. According to Henderson, these leaders also embrace the ethno-humanist and bureaucrat/administrator role identities (Lomotey, 1993).

In a 2021 *Educational Administration Quarterly* article, Rivera-McCutchen documents the successful administration of a Black male principal. She employs CRT and—in this qualitative study—creates a case study/ethnography using interviews, observations, and document review. Utilizing a *radical care framework*, she identifies important leadership components: (1) a focus on social justice, (2) authentic relationships, (3) belief in students and teachers, (4) navigating politics, and (5) radical hope.

J. Smith (2019), in a dissertation, provides narratives of six Black male principals who worked in predominantly White schools. These leaders stress: (1) the importance of family connections, (2) the need for power to impact social injustice, (3) the need for inclusive communities, and (4) an awareness that they were perceived as a threat to Whiteness.

Turbyfill (1997) interviewed three retired Black male principals who had served shortly after *Brown*. Not counterintuitively, the profiles stress the fact that these principals were community leaders—as were many Black male principals who served prior to and shortly after the *Brown* era (Siddle Walker, 2003).

*Case Studies.* Three of these studies (10%) are in the form of case studies (or multiple case studies), offering a more detailed glimpse of the leadership behavior of selected Black male principals (Brooks, 2017; Rivera-McCutchen, 2021; Turbyfill, 1997).

The Brooks dissertation (2017) is a case study. Additionally, the Rivera-McCutchen study (2021) is a case study. Turbyfill (1997) conducted case studies of three retired Black male principals. These three articles highlight the role of these men as community leaders and provide much information about their post-*Brown* leadership.

*Success Stories.* Three of the studies (10%) focus specifically on characteristics of successful Black male principals (Cramer, 2016; Rivera-McCutchen, 2021; Turner, 2014). Cramer (2016) discusses 12 successful Black male principals and considers strategies for retaining such leaders. This is a qualitative study in which he utilizes

CRT as the framework. The Rivera-McCutchen study (2021) is described above.

Writing a dissertation, Turner (2014) focuses on factors contributing to the academic success of Black male principals. These include: (1) availability of a support system, (2) adaptability, (3) compassion, (4) leadership, (5) ethics, (6) quality, and (7) relationships.

*Underrepresentation.* Two studies (7%) in this review deal with aspects of the underrepresentation of Black men in the principalship (Alston, 2018; Richardson, 2014). Alston's doctoral work (2018) focuses on racism in the practices of hiring elementary school principals and the consequential underrepresentation of Black males in the elementary school principalship. This study is qualitative, with interviews of eight Black male principals. Alston concludes that substantial, impactful barriers persist in limiting opportunities for prospective Black male principals.

Richardson (2014) produced a dissertation in which he focuses on the underrepresentation of Black male principals, using CRT— including counter-storytelling—and Self Efficacy Theory. In this qualitative study, he employs document review and interviews for data collection.

## *Discussion*

As is the case with research on Black women principals (and indeed with all principal research), most of the research on Black male principals has been published in dissertations. A plurality of the studies (10 of 29) explored aspects of the lived experiences (and associated challenges) of Black male principals. In four of these studies, the principals focus on issues of race, including advocating for social justice and acknowledging that they were perceived as a threat to Whiteness. Three studies highlight the principals' relationships with Black students, including a focus on the importance of mentoring these students. Principals in two of the studies emphasize a focus on student achievement, including understanding the principal's role as instructional leader.

Career aspirations are the focus of seven of the studies. The most consistent theme noted in these studies is the importance of support, role models, and mentors—learning from people around them. Leaders in these studies also stress the presence of obstacles, challenges, or barriers throughout their movement up the ladder. Other noted observations from Black male principals in these studies include: (1) the importance of transformational leadership, (2) confidence, and (3) acknowledgement of the rapidly decreasing number of Black male principals.

Commitment to students is a significant focus in six of the studies. In five of these, the Black male principals stress the importance of their focus on Black students, emphasizing positive relations, support, and mentoring.

Five of the studies focus on characteristics of Black male principals. The overwhelming theme in the findings of these studies are related to ethno-humanism (stressing larger community issues, authentic relationships, and the importance of family).

Three studies are case studies, and three studies display success stories of one or more Black male principals. The focus in the case studies is on the principals' role in the larger community and their relations with Black students. The success stories focus on factors contributing to the success of those leaders (e.g., compassion and mentoring) and strategies to retain such leaders. The last group of studies (2) focuses on the underrepresentation of Black males in the principalship.

## *Implications*

My interest herein is the persistent, pervasive, and disproportionate lack of success for most Black children in U.S. schools. I conducted the literature review for this chapter to ascertain what we know about the leadership of Black male principals, and further, to determine the extent to which that knowledge has implications for the improvement in the experiences of Black school children.

Black principals make a difference for Black students. Unfortunately, the most significant finding of this study is that we do not know very much about the leadership of Black (male) principals. Too few studies—with limited methodological approaches—have been done to date. We uncovered 29 studies of these leaders published between 1975 and 2021—45 years! All of them employ some form of qualitative research methodology. None pursue quantitative approaches in their explorations.

More than 80% of the studies were reported in dissertations. Given the extreme importance of Black male and female principals for students in general and Black students in particular, it appears that a renewed interest in research published in scholarly journals is needed to address these issues related to the leadership of Black (male) principals.

Given the extreme importance of Black male and female principals for students, in general, and Black students, in particular, it appears that an increased interest in scholarly—qualitative and quantitative—research to be published in journals is needed to address these issues related to the leadership of Black (male) principals. The qualitative research that has been done also opens the door for future theory-testing studies in this area.

The researchers in more than half of the studies reviewed herein utilize CRT to frame their explorations. This is indeed encouraging given that CRT has been shown to be a sound, demanding, and thorough vehicle through which one can better understand and analyze data. Generally, CRT enables us to describe and understand the impact of race in society. More particularly in this work, it allows us to communicate and comprehend the impact of race—and racism—on the leadership of Black (male) principals and on their interactions with Black students.

A focus on the lived experiences of Black male principals is the theme of one in three of the studies reviewed herein. More research needs to be done in this area, as several factors significantly impact the lived experiences of these leaders, including—as I have shown—race and racism.

Given my primary interest in Black student success, it is somewhat reassuring to note that the researchers in one in five of the studies reviewed herein look at the commitment of Black male principals to Black students. This is an area that is promising and should be explored more. A similar number of the researchers whose work I looked at center on aspirations of (1) individuals seeking principalships, and/or (2) then-current Black male principals.

We learn most from the successes of leaders (though we can also learn from their failures). Only three of the studies reported on in this review emphasize the qualities of successful Black male principals; more work is needed in this area.

I noted earlier the wide-scale shortage of Black male principals in U.S. schools. It is disappointingly noticeable that only two of the studies reported on herein focus on the shortage of Black male principals. Scholars interested in this area should contribute to this limited research.

## *Conclusion*

The reader is reminded that my focus is on the success of Black students. While there is some valuable information in the pages of these 29 studies that I reviewed, there is little information that is overwhelmingly useful in addressing this quagmire.

The extensive use of CRT in these studies is, in one regard, reassuring. For too long we have focused on genetics and, more recently, on the opportunity gap as primary explanations for the limited success of Black students in U.S. schools. This emergence in the 1980s of an increased cognizance of the significance of race and racism in understanding racial disparities, in general, and the limited success of Black students is promising. It seems to be a significant step in addressing issues of race, racism in schools, and institutionalized White supremacy.

Also promising is the focus in the research on the lived experiences of Black male principals and the commitment of these leaders to Black students. Underexplored areas include the shortage of Black male principals. This is a critical research focus if we are to see the success levels of Black students improve appreciably in the future.

We can and will do a better job of ensuring the substantially improved success of Black students in U.S. schools. Research has been shown to be of significance in bringing about improvements in education and of impacting policy. Accordingly, we must redouble our efforts in studying the factors that hold back these students from being more successful. Herein lies my challenge to researchers—Blacks and others—to address these factors, including the all-important leadership of Black (male) principals.

## *Discussion Questions*

1.  There are nearly twice as many studies looking at the leadership of Black women principals as there are studies exploring Black male principal leadership. (There are 55 studies of Black women principals as compared to 29 studies of Black male principals.) Consider why this is the case.

2.  Juxtapose the findings in Chapter 4 related to Black women principals with those in this chapter on Black male principals. How are the findings similar? How are they different? What are the implications of the similarities and the differences?

3.  Of the 29 studies discussed in this review, 16 (55%) employed critical race theory in their analyses. Discuss why you think so many researchers of Black male principals would choose to use this framework?

4.  We do not know very much about the leadership of Black principals. What do you think may be the cause of this lack of information?

# References

Adkins-Sharif, J. (2020). *The racial challenges facing Black male school leaders enacting social justice agendas in environments of privilege* [Unpublished doctoral dissertation]. University of Massachusetts, Boston.

Alston, K. R. (2018). *Examining the impact of race in the recruitment, placement, and retention of African-American male principals in rural North Carolina school districts: a qualitative study of the perceptions of African-American male principals serving in rural, high-poverty, high-minority elementary schools* [Unpublished doctoral dissertation]. North Carolina State University.

Anderson, R. (2015). *Staff perceptions of African-American male principals.* LAP LAMBERT Academic Publishing.

Banks, E. M. (1975). Career aspirations of Black male principals in large northeastern Ohio cities. *Dissertation Abstracts International Section A: Humanities and Social Sciences, 35*(11-A), 6958.

Bell, D. A. (1995). Who's afraid of critical race theory? *University of Illinois Law Review, 893*(4).

Black, W. J. (2012). *Characteristics and obstacles: The rise of African American male principals in Texas* [Unpublished doctoral dissertation]. University of Texas, San Antonio.

Bridges, E. M. (1982). Research on the school administrator: The state of the art, 1967–1980. *Educational Administration Quarterly, 18*(3), 12–33.

Brooks, A. E. (2017). *A study of lived experiences of African American male principals in urban elementary schools* [Unpublished doctoral dissertation]. Bellarmine University.

Carter-Oliver, C. C. (2014). Stories of African American male principals following the intra district desegregation plan [Unpublished doctoral dissertation]. University of Missouri-St. Louis.

Cramer, T. L. (2016). *An analysis of effective and experienced African-American male principal retention in a large suburban/urban school district* [Unpublished doctoral dissertation]. University of Pennsylvania.

Crenshaw, K., Gotanda, N., & Peller, G., & Thomas, K. (1995). *Critical race theory: The key writings that formed the movement.* The New Press.

Delgado, R., & Stefanic, J. (2012). *Critical race theory: An introduction.* New York University Press.

Derrick, L. (2009). *Exploring mentoring relationships between African American high school males and African American male principals* [Unpublished doctoral dissertation]. Bowling Green State University. http://rave.ohiolink.edu/etdc/view?acc_num=bgsu1245425360

Dunbar, J. N. (2015). *African-American males, African-American female principals, and the opportunity gap* [Unpublished doctoral dissertation]. Georgia Southern University.

Funchess, M. (2014). *Ethical decision making of African American male principals: Values and professional responsibilities* [Unpublished doctoral dissertation]. University of Redlands.

Grubbs, C. (2021). *The lived experiences of Black male principals in urban settings* [Unpublished doctoral dissertation]. Youngstown State University.

Henderson, G. D. (2015). Leadership experiences of African American male secondary urban principals: The impact of beliefs, values, and experiences on school leadership practices. *Journal of African American Males in Education, 6*(2), 38–54.

Humphrey, D. L. (2007). *Career development of African American male high school principals* [Unpublished doctoral dissertation]. University of Georgia.

Jackson, S. (2018). *The principal pipeline: A qualitative exploration of strategies for the recruitment and retention of Black male public school principals* [Unpublished doctoral dissertation]. St. John Fisher College.

Johnson, C. (2018). *Resiliency of African American principals in K–12 education* [Unpublished doctoral dissertation]. University of La Verne.

Ladson-Billings, G., & Tate, B. (1995). Toward a critical race theory of education. *Teachers College Record, 97*(1), 47–68.

Lomotey, K. (1990). Introduction. In K. Lomotey (Ed.), *Going to school: The African-American experience* (pp. 1–9). State University of New York Press.

Lomotey, K. (1993). African American principals: Bureaucrat/administrators and ethno-humanists. *Urban Education, 27*(4), 395–412.

Lomotey, K. (2019). Research on the leadership of Black women principals: Implications for Black students. *Educational Researcher, 48*(6), 336–348.

Lomotey, K. (in press). Institutionalized white racism: The impact on U.S. higher education. In K. Lomotey & W. Smith (Eds.), *The racial crisis in American higher education: Continuing dilemmas, ongoing setbacks and new challenges.* State University of New York Press.

Lynn, M., Davis, L. P., Hughes, R., Giles, M., Warren, C., Stovall, D., Davila, E., Dixson, A., Aleman, E., and Flowers, N. (2020). *Critical race theory in education scholars respond to Executive Memo M-20-34.* Medium. https://medium.com/@addixson_5047/critical-race-theory-and-education-scholars-respond-executive-memo-m-20-34-a8b80a3445f0

Miller, D. A. (2019). *"Their story, through their eyes": Factors impacting African American male principals* [Unpublished doctoral dissertation]. California State University, Fresno.

Miller, M. A. (2008). *A study of the career paths and leadership of male principals in the elementary schools of Ohio* [Unpublished doctoral dissertation]. Bowling Green State University.

Moultry, E. G. (2014). *Four African American male principals and their leadership in urban elementary schools* [Unpublished doctoral dissertation]. Texas A&M University.

Palija, L. (2020). *The study of Black American male school principals' life experiences and how they affect Black American male students in their schools to close the academic achievement gap* [Unpublished doctoral dissertation]. National Louis University.

Parker, L., & Lynn, M. (2002). What's race got to do with it? Critical race theory's conflicts with and connections to qualitative research methodology and epistemology. *Qualitative Inquiry, 8,* 7–22.

Richardson, R. E. (2014). *Creating internal and external support systems for African American male aspiring principals: The evolution of the African American male principal.* [Unpublished doctoral dissertation]. California State University, East Bay.

Rivera-McCutchen, R. L. (2021). "We don't got time for grumbling": Toward an ethic of radical care in urban school leadership. *Educational Administration Quarterly, 57*(2), 257–289.

Siddle Walker, V. (2003). The architects of Black schooling in the segregated South: The case of one principal leader. *Journal of Curriculum and Supervision, 19,* 54–72.

Smith, J. (2019). *The racial encounters of Black male principals who lead predominately white K–12 public schools in Commonwealth of Massachusetts* [Unpublished doctoral dissertation]. Northeastern University.

Smith, P. A. (2019). *Leading while Black and male: A phenomenology of Black male school leadership* [Unpublished doctoral dissertation]. Columbia University.

Smith, P. A. (2021). Black male school leaders: Protectors and defenders of children, community, culture and village. *Journal of School Leadership, 31*(1–2), 29–49.

Thomas, M. J. (2018). *Guess who's coming to dinner: How African American administrators in predominantly white educational systems negotiate cultural sacrifice* [Unpublished doctoral dissertation]. University of St. Thomas.

Tillman, L. (2004). African American principals and the legacy of *Brown*. *Review of Research in Education, 28*, 101–146.

Turbyfill, R. L. (1997). *Understanding the leadership of desegregated schools through the life stories of retired male African-American principals* [Unpublished doctoral dissertation]. University of North Carolina, Greensboro.

Turner, R. C. (2014). *Factors influencing the academic achievement and success of African American male principals in a midsouth state* [Unpublished doctoral dissertation]. University of Arkansas.

U.S. Equal Employment Opportunity Commission. (2018). *Job patterns for minorities and women in elementary-secondary public schools (EEO-5).* https://www.eeoc.gov/statistics/job-patterns-minorities-and-women-elementary-secondary-public-schools-eeo-5

Washington, T. (2019). *The impact of African American male principals on African-American male students in two all-male urban schools* [Unpublished doctoral dissertation]. George Mason University.

# APPENDIX

## *Studies Reviewed in Chapter 5*

Adkins-Sharif, J. (2020). *The racial challenges facing Black male school leaders enacting social justice agendas in environments of privilege* [Unpublished doctoral dissertation]. University of Massachusetts, Boston.

Alston, K. R. (2018). *Examining the impact of race in the recruitment, placement, and retention of African- American male principals in rural North Carolina school districts: A qualitative study of the perceptions of African-American Male principals serving in rural, high-poverty, high-minority elementary schools* [Unpublished doctoral dissertation]. North Carolina State University.

Anderson, R. (2015). *Staff perceptions of African-American male principals.* LAP LAMBERT Academic Publishing.

Banks, E. M. (1975). Career aspirations of Black male principals in large northeastern Ohio cities. *Dissertation Abstracts International Section A: Humanities and Social Sciences, 35*(11-A), 6958.

Black, W. J. (2012). *Characteristics and obstacles: The rise of African American male principals in Texas.* [Unpublished doctoral dissertation]. University of Texas, San Antonio.

Brooks, A. E. (2017). *A study of lived experiences of African American male principals in urban elementary schools* [Unpublished doctoral dissertation]. Bellarmine University.

Carter-Oliver, C. C. (2014). *Stories of African American male principals following the intra district desegregation plan* [Unpublished doctoral dissertation]. University of Missouri-St. Louis.

Cramer, T. L. (2016). *An analysis of effective and experienced African-American male principal retention in a large suburban/urban school district* [Unpublished doctoral dissertation]. University of Pennsylvania.

Dawson, N. C. (2018). *Our brothers' keeper: The leadership practices of African American male principals and their work with African American male students in rural schools* [Unpublished doctoral dissertation]. University of North Carolina, Greensboro.

Derrick, L. (2009). *Exploring mentoring relationships between African American high school males and African American male principals*

[Unpublished doctoral dissertation]. Bowling Green State University. http://rave.ohiolink.edu/etdc/view?acc_num=bgsu1245425360

Funchess, M. (2014). *Ethical decision making of African American male principals: Values and professional responsibilities* [Unpublished doctoral dissertation]. University of Redlands.

Grubbs, C. (2021). *The lived experiences of Black male principals in urban settings* [Unpublished doctoral dissertation]. Youngstown State University.

Henderson, G. D. (2015). Leadership experiences of African American male secondary urban principals: The impact of beliefs, values, and experiences on school leadership practices. *Journal of African American Males in Education, 6*(2), 38–54.

Humphrey, D. L. (2007). *Career development of African American male high school principals* [Unpublished doctoral dissertation]. University of Georgia.

Jackson, S. (2018). *The principal pipeline: A qualitative exploration of strategies for the recruitment and retention of Black male public school principals* [Unpublished doctoral dissertation]. St. John Fisher College.

Johnson, C. (2018). *Resiliency of African American principals in K–12 education* [Unpublished doctoral dissertation]. University of La Verne.

Miller, D. A. (2019). *"Their story, through their eyes": Factors impacting African American male principals* [Unpublished doctoral dissertation]. California State University, Fresno.

Miller, M. A. (2008). *A study of the career paths and leadership of male principals in the elementary schools of Ohio* [Unpublished doctoral dissertation]. Bowling Green State University.

Moultry, E. G. (2014). *Four African American male principals and their leadership in urban elementary schools* [Unpublished doctoral dissertation]. Texas A&M University.

Palija, L. (20290). *The study of Black American male school principals' life experiences and how they affect Black American male students in their schools to close the academic achievement gap* [Unpublished doctoral dissertation]. National Louis University.

Richardson, R. E. (2014). *Creating internal and external support systems for African American male aspiring principals: The evolution of the African American male principal* [Unpublished doctoral dissertation]. California State University, East Bay.

Rivera-McCutchen, R. L. (2021). "We don't got time for grumbling": Toward an ethic of radical care in urban school leadership. *Educational Administration Quarterly, 57*(2), 257–289.

Smith, J. (2019). *The racial encounters of Black male principals who lead predominately white K–12 public schools in Commonwealth of Massachusetts* [Unpublished doctoral dissertation]. Northeastern University.

Smith, P. A. (2019). *Leading while Black and male: A phenomenology of Black male school leadership* [Unpublished doctoral dissertation]. Columbia University.

Smith, P. A. (2021). Black male school leaders: Protectors and defenders of children, community, culture and village. *Journal of School Leadership, 31*(1–2), 29–49.

Thomas, M. J. (2018). *Guess who's coming to dinner: How African American administrators in predominantly white educational systems negotiate cultural sacrifice* [Unpublished doctoral dissertation]. University of St. Thomas.

Turbyfill, R. L. (1997). *Understanding the leadership of desegregated schools through the life stories of retired male African-American principals* [Unpublished doctoral dissertation]. University of North Carolina, Greensboro.

Turner, R. C. (2014). *Factors influencing the academic achievement and success of African American male principals in a midsouth state* [Unpublished doctoral dissertation]. University of Arkansas.

Washington, T. (2019). *The impact of African American male principals on African-American male students in two all-male urban schools* [Unpublished doctoral dissertation]. George Mason University Press.

# PART THREE:
## Justice for Black Students (and People): Ethno-Humanism and Cultural Responsiveness

# 6.

# ETHNO-HUMANISM: EXTENDING ITS SIGNIFICANCE

I have researched and written about Black principals for more than 50 years. Early in my work, I found three qualities possessed by successful Black principals who contribute to Black student success. These are: (1) confidence in the ability of all students to be successful, (2) commitment to the success of all children, and (3) compassion for all students, their families, and their communities. In this chapter, I discuss the significance of this role identity, consider the contributions of other scholars to this discussion, and conclude by looking at the significance of this work.

## *The Three C's*

Recall that in earlier writings (Lomotey, 1985, 1989) I asked, what qualities do successful Black principals hold in common with each other? Through observations of three successful Black elementary school principals, interviews of these same principals, interviews of teachers in their charge, and document review, I uncovered three qualities that these successful Black principals held in common: confidence, commitment, and compassion. During the observations, the principals displayed these qualities in their interactions with teachers, students, parents, and community members. In my discussions with each principal, they exuded a sincere and focused dedication to their role as principal—in part through articulating a vision that embodied their dedication to these characteristics.

Moreover, teachers were constantly acknowledging the presence of these qualities in their principals.

These qualities, of course, are not all that principals need to be successful in leading schools wherein students are academically, socially, culturally, and spiritually successful. Still, they are critically important characteristics for several reasons. We know that successful principals interact with students, teachers, parents, and community members; they do not spend the bulk of their workday in their offices. They engage members of the school family in classrooms, in hallways, in the cafeteria, in the gym, on and near school buses, in the schoolyard, and in the larger community.

Why are the confidence, commitment, and compassion of successful Black principals so critical for Black children? These leaders are important adult figures exuding confidence in the ability of all children to do well academically. This is important; children need to interact with caring adults who display faith in their potential to be successful. If they see adults who have confidence in their potential, they are more likely to do well academically, socially, culturally, and spiritually.

When students observe their school leaders exhibiting dedication to their success, they are more likely to gain added commitment to their *own* success—and to ultimately do better academically, socially, culturally, and spiritually.

Compassion is the recognition of one's circumstances—whatever they may be—and acting to help the individual advance to the next level. Imagine an individual with the influence of a school principal displaying such concern, not only for their students, but for their students' families and communities; there is a tremendous amount of potential there, not only in terms of moving the students forward individually and collectively, but also in terms of moving families and communities forward. Collectively, confidence, commitment, and compassion are extremely powerful qualities that, when exhibited by a principal, catapult students in potential and realized levels of success. Laura Robbins wrote about one such principal.

Robbins (2022) penned an article titled "A Black School Principal Changed My Life. Here's Why We Need Black People in Positions of Power." It is the story of a Black girl's experience in an overwhelmingly White elementary school; she learned that her principal, Jackie Scott, was a "strong unapologetically Black woman." Robbins says, "Jackie Scott was a legend; she greeted every kid at the door in the morning, attended every away soccer game, and was interviewed more than once by the Boston Globe." At another point, Robbins says, "The example set for me by Jackie was a lasting and powerful one. Despite the messaging I got on television and in our history books, because of her, it rarely occurred to me that there were limitations to what I could do or be." In another quote from Robbins, "What would my life have been like if our principal, like all of our students, had been White? Would I have known that my brown skin was something to be proud of and my kinky hair was a crown to be worn with dignity." While there are not explicit indications of Scotts display of the three C's, it is clear that Robbins felt the confidence, commitment, and compassion of Principal Scott.

There is a clear cultural significance to the three C's. I turn again to Shujaa's (1993) notion of *education versus schooling*. Education is an instrument for intergenerational diffusion of cultural identity through awareness of the morals, convictions, conventions, norms, traditions, and sensibilities that have enabled a people to endure. Education is acquiring knowledge and internalizing one's own cultural standards. It transpires in formal and informal venues. It provides the ability for individuals within a group to successfully interact within the family, community, and race and to preserve the integrity of their own culture (Shujaa, 1993). Successful Black principals displaying this confidence, commitment, and compassion are clearly providing cultural reinforcement for their students.

These three C's are also reminiscent of the way in which Black women principals are often described in the literature, particularly as it relates to othermothering, caring, and nurturing (Carson, 2017; Case, 1997; Dillard, 1995; Loder, 2005; Lomotey, 2019). The descriptions of these three C's and the descriptions that researchers provide of Black women principals caring, nurturing, and othermothering often overlap. In 1993, I first used the term ethno-humanism to encompass the three C's (Lomotey, 1993; Chapter 3 herein).

## Research on Ethno-Humanism

The related works of several authors followed my initial introduction of the ethno-humanist role identity (as well as the bureaucrat/administrator role identity). A few researchers describe aspects of ethno-humanism—some by name (e.g., Dawson, 2018; Dunbar, 2015) and others by merely describing components of the ethno-humanist role identity (e.g., Dillard, 1995; Lyman, 2000).

Some researchers who have utilized the term ethno-humanism to describe the leadership of Black principals include Tillman (2004), Dawson (2018), Khalifa et al. (2019), Dunbar (2015), Henderson (2015), Weaver (2009), and Gooden (2005).

Selected authors who describe aspects of ethno-humanism without using the term include Rivera-McCutchen (2020), Lyman (2000), Dillard (1995), Reitzug and Patterson (1998), Lightfoot (1983) and Siddle Walker (1993a, 1993b, 1996, 2003).

## Authors Utilizing the Term Ethno-Humanism

Khalifa et al. (2019), in a comprehensive exploration of literature on decolonizing and Indigenous ways of leading, argue that the ethno-humanist role identity can be used to retain a group's culture amid chaos. Dawson (2018), in a qualitative dissertation utilizing CRT and exploring the relationship between Black male principals and Black male students, highlights the role of these principals in supporting Black male students. In this study, the author's illustrations of this support include encouraging positive relationships and noting exclusionary disciplinary practices. Dawson uses the

ETHNO-HUMANISM

ethno-humanist role identity in the analysis, as well as the bureaucrat/administrator role identity.

In her dissertation, Dunbar (2015) looks at the opportunity gap between Black males and Black women seeking principalships. Conducting interviews of three Black women principals, she discusses the impact of barriers, leadership style, and gender on their ascension to the principalship. Dunbar goes on to stress the importance of ethno-humanism, using CRT; these principals demonstrated and relied upon the three C's in their leadership.

Looking at the significance of several characteristics, including experiences, values, and beliefs, Henderson (2015) interviewed six Black male principals. The principals address broad social and systemic issues and displayed integrated leadership styles. Henderson noted that these Black male principals effectively displayed the ethno-humanist role identity as well as the bureaucrat/administrator role identity. He suggests that professional development efforts should focus on these two role identities.

Weaver (2009) utilized ethno-humanism as a part of a theoretical basis in looking at Black principals' attitudes toward culturally responsive pedagogy/teaching and culturally responsive school leadership. Initially, the principals had limited knowledge of culturally responsive pedagogy/teaching and culturally responsive school leadership—though they thought that both were important. In utilizing ethno-humanism in this dissertation, Weaver explored this role identity not just with principals, but also with teachers. While this is a logical and, perhaps, obvious use of the three C's, I am aware of no other work wherein this role identity has been applied to teachers.

Gooden (2005) conducted a case study of a Black principal of an information technology high school. In his analysis of this case study, Gooden noted that the principal combined traditional ideas of leadership with ethno-humanism to account for changing times and circumstances. Gooden contrasts the ethno-humanist role identity with the bureaucrat/administrator role identity, noting that the principal used both.

In a 2014 dissertation, Wilkerson observed four Black male principals, noting their experiences in "high-priority" schools. In studying the principals in these turnaround schools, he utilized the ethno-humanism role identity as a theme. In discussing the increasing diversity in urban schools, he described what he called "the browning of the student body." Wilkerson continues, citing Henderson (2015), discussing the ethno-humanism that successful Black principals display—often to "the detriment of the leader himself" (p. 121). Wilkerson speaks specifically about not only ethno-humanism, but also the bureaucrat/administrator role identity.

Wilson (2020) conducted a comparative case study, using focus groups and interviews, to explore the leadership of 10 Black principals. He focused on the lived experiences of those leaders. Referring to Henderson's work (2015), Wilson draws upon the ethno-humanist role identity in the analysis.

Finally, Tillman (2004)—in her landmark literature review on Black principals and *Brown v. Board of Education*—focuses on pushing for the re-establishment of the more comprehensive, meaningful, and substantive role that Black principals played prior to *Brown*. Throughout her analysis, Tillman highlights and emphasizes the ethno-humanist role identity. A plethora of research on Black principals is included in this review, which is pregnant with insights and significance.

## *Authors Using Selected Components of Ethno-humanism Without Naming It*

Rivera-McCutchen (2020) conducted a case study of a successful Black male urban school principal. She classifies five key leadership components into what she refers to as a *radical care framework*. Much of what is encompassed in ethno-humanism appears in McCutchen's framework. She recommends incorporating the components of her radical care framework in professional development for principals.

ETHNO-HUMANISM                                    129

Lyman (2000) assessed the leadership of Kenneth Hinton, the principal of an early childhood educational center. Hinton displayed the three C's (Tillman, 2004) when interacting with students and other members of the school community. Dillard (1995) describes Gloria Nathan, a Black woman who served as a high school principal. Nathan felt personally responsible for the academic, social, cultural, and spiritual success of her students: commitment to the success of all students (Tillman, 2004).

Reitzug and Patterson (1998) studied the leadership of Debbie Pressley, a Black woman middle school principal. Pressley was committed to her students' education and often interacted with students' family members and other members of the larger community: commitment to the education of all children (Tillman, 2004).

Lightfoot (1983) describes George Washington Carver Comprehensive High School in Atlanta and the school's leader, Principal Logan. She discusses the principal's belief that educators should expect all students to excel. This principal stressed the importance of high standards with teachers and students. Here we see one aspect of ethno-humanism at play: confidence in the ability of all students to succeed (Tillman, 2004).

Siddle Walker (1993a,1993b, 1996, 2003) describes Nicholas Longworth Dillard, the principal of Caswell County Training School. Dillard displayed his commitment to his students' overall success. He viewed the success of every student as priority one: commitment to the success of all children (Tillman, 2004).

## *Assessing the Research*

What does the work that others have done related to the ethno-humanist—and bureaucrat/administrator—role identities tell us? Khalifa et al. (2019) highlight the role of ethno-humanism in reinforcing the culture of students. If we are concerned, not just with the academic success of Black students, but also with their social, cultural, and spiritual success, a role identity that, it is argued, reinforces a student's culture is worthy of further study. The significance of this cultural reinforcement is illustrated in the words of Shujaa (1993) described earlier.

Several of these authors utilized ethno-humanism in their work as a component of their framework to assess the leadership of the Black principals (Dawson, 2018; Weaver, 2009; Wilkerson, 2014; Wilson, 2020). The authors of a few of the studies looking at ethno-humanism also considered the significance of the bureaucrat/administrator role identity, and in some instances juxtaposed and compared the two role identities (Henderson, 2015; Dawson, 2018; Gooden, 2005; Wilkerson, 2014).

Three researchers used CRT to evaluate the leadership of their subjects (Dawson, 2018; Dunbar, 2015; Rivera-McCutchen, 2020). While this is not most of the studies, it is a plurality. CRT was used widely in the studies that I reviewed on Black male principals (Chapter 5 herein). A total of 16 (or 55%) of the 29 studies used CRT. Of the 55 studies reviewed in my research on Black women principals (2019; Chapter 4 herein), five (9%) used CRT in their analysis.

Some researchers stress how Black principals in their studies valued the ethno-humanist role identity (Dunbar, 2015). Henderson (2015) and Rivera-McCutchen (2020) emphasize the need for professional development programs for (aspiring) principals to focus on the three C's. Weaver (2009) discusses ethno-humanism not just as a key role identity of successful Black principals, but also as a valuable characteristic of Black *teachers*. This, to my knowledge, is a novel—though worthy—idea.

Many of the researchers who did not use the term ethno-humanism, also provide valuable data. Several authors emphasize all the three C's (Rivera-McCutchen, 2020; Lyman, 2000). Others emphasize one or two components of the ethno-humanist role identity.

## Final Thoughts

Ethno-humanism is an important characteristic of successful Black principals. A large percentage of studies in which researchers investigate the leadership of successful Black principals show these leaders displaying some or all the three Cs: confidence, commitment, and compassion. In some instances, the role identity is spelled out, and in others it is implied.

Considering my interest in the academic, social, cultural, and spiritual success of Black students, I would echo the call for principal preparation programs and in-service professional development programs incorporating discussions of the importance of leaders displaying confidence, commitment, and compassion for all students. There are a variety of pedagogical approaches that can be used in such professional development forums. These include: (1) large and small group discussions, (2) videotapes of lectures and demonstrations of leaders displaying the three Cs, (3) skits with participants depicting these characteristics, (4) observations of successful principals at work, and much, much more.

The ethno-humanist role identity has been shown to be an important quality displayed by successful Black principals. In our quest to bring about greater academic, social, cultural, and spiritual success for Black children, it is important that we highlight and encourage the implementation of these and other qualities of successful Black principals.

## Discussion Questions

1.  Given the unique leadership of successful Black women principals, as described by Dillard (1995), Loder (2005), and others, how, if at all, do Black male principals and Black female principals display the ethno-humanist role identity differently based upon their gender?

2. If ethno-humanism is not all that Black principals need to be successful, what other qualities might be of value for these leaders? Relatedly, what other qualities do successful Black principals hold in common with each other?

3. In what specific ways can successful Black principals display the three components of the ethno-humanist role identity: confidence, commitment, and compassion?

4. Discuss the significance of Weaver's (2019) unique application of the ethno-humanist role identity to the work of teachers.

# *References*

Carson, D. (2017). *What are the experiences of African American female principals in high poverty urban schools?* [Unpublished doctoral dissertation]. University of North Texas.

Case, K. I. (1997). African American othermothering in the urban elementary school. *Urban Review, 29*(1), 25–39.

Dawson, N. C. (2018). *Our brothers' keeper: The leadership practices of African American male principals and their work with African American male students in rural schools* [Unpublished doctoral dissertation]. University of North Carolina, Greensboro.

Dillard, C. B. (1995). Leading with her life: An African American feminist (re)interpretation of leadership for an urban high school principal. *Educational Administration Quarterly, 31*(4), 539–563.

Dunbar, J. N. (2015). *African American males, African American female principals and the opportunity gap* [Unpublished doctoral dissertation]. Georgia Southern University.

Gooden, M. (2005). The role of an African American principal in an urban information technology high school. *Educational Administration Quarterly, 41*(4), 630–650.

Henderson, G. (2015). Leadership experiences of African American male secondary urban principals: The impact of beliefs, values, and experiences on school leadership practices. *Journal of African American Males in Education, 6*(2), 38–54.

Khalifa, M. A., Khalil, D., Marsh, T.E., & Halloran, C. (2019). Toward an indigenous, decolonizing school leadership: A literature review. *Educational Administration Quarterly, 55*(4), 571–614.

Lightfoot, S. L. (1983). *The good high school: Portraits of character and culture.* Basic Books.

Loder, T. L. (2005). African American women principals' reflections on social change, community, othermothering, and Chicago public school reform. *Urban Education, 40*(3), 298–320.

Lomotey, K. (1985). *Black principals in Black elementary schools: School leadership and school success* [Unpublished doctoral dissertation]. Stanford University.

Lomotey, K. (1989). *African-American principals: School leadership and success.* Praeger.

Lomotey, K. (1993). African-American principals: Bureaucrat/administrators and ethno-humanists. *Urban Education, 27*(4), 395–412.

Lomotey, K. (2019). Research on the leadership of Black women principals: Implications for Black students. *Educational Researcher, 48*(6), 336–348

Lyman, L. (2000). *How do they know you care? The principal's challenge.* Teachers College Press.

Reitzug, U. C., & Patterson, J. (1998). "I'm not going to lose you!" Empowerment through caring in an urban principal's practice with students. *Urban Education, 33*, 150–181.

Rivera-McCutchen, R. L. (2020). "We don't got time for grumbling." Toward an ethic of radical care in urban school leadership. *Educational Administration Quarterly, 57*(2), 257–289.

Robbins, L. C. (2022, February 14). *A Black school principal changed my life. Here's why we need Black people in positions of power.* Huffpost. https://www.huffpost.com/entry/brian-flores-black-school-principal-leade r_n_6206dcfbe4b04af87f3d2e28

Shujaa, M. J. (1993). Education and schooling: You can have one without the other. *Urban Education, 27*(4), 328–351.

Siddle Walker, V. (1993a). Caswell County Training School, 1933–1969: Relationships between community and school. *Harvard Educational Review, 63*, 161–182.

Siddle Walker, V. (1993b). Interpersonal caring in the "good" segregated schooling of African-American children: Evidence from the Case of the Caswell County Training School. *Urban Review, 25*, 63–77.

Siddle Walker, V. (1996). *Their highest potential: An African American school community in the segregated South.* University of North Carolina Press.

Siddle Walker, V. (2003). The architects of Black schooling in the segregated South: The case of one principal leader. *Journal of Curriculum and Supervision, 19,* 54–72.

Tillman, L. C. (2004). African American principals and the legacy of Brown. *Review of Research in Education, 28,* 101–146.

Weaver, T. L. (2009). *Principals' attitudes toward the use of culturally relevant pedagogy and culturally responsive leadership in predominantly African American schools* [Unpublished doctoral dissertation]. Florida Atlantic University.

Wilkerson, R. D. (2014). *Invisible to visible, unheard to heard: African American principals leading high priority schools in North Carolina* [Unpublished doctoral dissertation]. University of North Carolina, Greensboro.

Wilson, E. E. (2020). *Perceptions: A comparative case study of the lived experiences of urban and suburban African American administrators* [Unpublished doctoral dissertation]. Seton Hall University.

# 7.

# CULTURALLY RESPONSIVE PEDAGOGY/TEACHING

## *Introduction*

Culturally responsive pedagogy/teaching (CRP/T) is extremely important for Black students and for all students. I use CRP/T to include what I see as very similar terms, including culturally relevant teaching, culturally relevant pedagogy, culturally responsive teaching, and culturally responsive pedagogy. In each instance, the focus is on designing classrooms and schools that emphasize the culture of the learner. It increases the likelihood that students will effectively engage in the teaching/learning process through receiving and internalizing the content of the curriculum. It ensures that the pedagogical and cultural focus within the classroom is responsive to—and addresses— the culture of the learner. In the present context, Black students must be able to see themselves in the curriculum.

In this chapter, I focus on CRP/T, its importance for Black students, and the relationship between CRP/T and ethno-humanism. I begin with a brief historical sketch and key assumptions related to CRP/T. From there, I discuss the relationship between CRP/T and ethno-humanism. Finally, I consider what this discussion means for Black students—and Black people.

## *Historical Sketch*

The earliest references to CRP/T were seen more than 20 years ago (Foster, 1995; Ladson-Billings, 1994). Many of the initial writers in this area noted that this concept has three foci: academic achievement, competence, and sociopolitical consciousness. That is, if CRP/T is effective, it must successfully (1) focus on the academic achievement of students; (2) address the overall competence of students; and (3) enable students to see and understand inequity and social injustice within society.

The seminal work of Geneva Gay (2010) highlights the practical aspect of what teachers can do in the classroom to display CRP/T: tactics and procedures. Ladson-Billings (1994) defined CRP/T as "a pedagogy that empowers students intellectually, socially, emotionally, and politically by using cultural referents to impart knowledge, skills, and attitudes" (p. 18). The inclination, too often, is on disempowering students—particularly Black and other historically marginalized students—and minimizing the opportunities for them to be successful academically, socially, culturally, and spiritually. The notion of empowering students is critically important.

## *Assumptions*

There are several assumptions associated with displaying CRP/T. To effectively offer CRP/T, these assumptions must be in place. They include:

- Acknowledging group *similarities* and *variations*;

- Supporting groups other than one's own, employing critical self-reflection;

- Eliminating the use of deficit analyses and, instead, building upon what students know—what they bring to the table;

- Understanding that education is, by definition, cultural;

- Acknowledging that all students should have some teachers and school leaders who look like them; and

- For many, making a revolutionary shift in thinking—and behavior.

We must be cognizant of the fact that there are different cultural and racial groups within our student populations. (Moreover, students differ by class, gender, sexual orientation, height, weight, "beauty," ableism, and other illegitimate vehicles for oppression and exclusion.)

To practice CRP/T, a teacher must be cognizant of the fact that each cultural group brings unique characteristics (e.g., language or dialect, dress, and foods) while there are, at the same time, many common characteristics that are shared by groups. The differences, by definition, have an impact on our interactions. Acknowledging this is an important step in avoiding evaluating and comparing cultural differences and concluding that one characteristic or set of characteristics—and by extension, one group—is superior to another.

To be supportive of groups other than one's own, educators must employ critical self-reflection. Critical self-reflection refers to the practice of interrogating our personal beliefs, premises, and sensemaking. We partake in critical self-reflection in two stages: investigation and verbalization.

Indeed, our success in teaching students is a result of how we feel about them; what we believe drives what we do. What we value propels and determines what we do in the classroom. We must reflect on: (1) how we feel about Black students and students from other groups, and (2) our thoughts about education in general. According to Howard (2010), teachers must consider issues of race and culture to be able to successfully practice CRP/T. As educators, we must examine our personal cultural norms and our institutional norms to ascertain how they contribute to—or detract from—our efforts to enable Black children and all children to be successful. We cannot, for example, effectively engage in the teaching/learning process if we do not acknowledge, understand, respect, and embrace the culture of Black people, reflected in our Black students.

Because children bring differences related to race, class, gender, religion, sexual orientation, abledness, and more into the classroom, as teachers, we must acknowledge those differences. We must be committed to developing our individual cultural competence:

knowledge of the particularities of each child in our classroom. Only by gaining and internalizing this cultural knowledge can we begin to address the cultural needs of Black students and all students. Respect of and valuing difference are the next steps, and only by acknowledging and understanding a group's particularities can we begin to respect and value them. We must value education for Black children and for all children.

A commitment to the education of Black children or children from any group necessitates avoiding deficit analyses. We must evaluate students with a focus on their strengths. Gay (2010) advises that, when teachers employ a deficit-based view, the language, background, and distinctiveness of the students serve as obstacles to successful outcomes. Foster (1995) notes that Black teachers can successfully employ CRP/T in part because of a sense of connection, attachment, and camaraderie with Black students. A focus on strengths matters.

Consider, for example, Black English or the Ebonics dialect. The way that a teacher introduces so-called Standard English to a Black speaker of Ebonics goes a long way in terms of the success of the teaching/learning process. Belittling a Black child who speaks Ebonics suggests—directly or indirectly—that Ebonics is inferior to Standard English. Employing such a focus is less likely to bring about success in the teaching/learning process. Conversely, if a teacher approaches this lesson by stressing that *in teaching Standard English, we are building upon the strengths that the student already possesses,* the Black student is significantly more likely to be responsive—and the teaching/learning process is more likely to be successful. Building on any student's strength is significantly more effective than focusing on your perception of the limitations or deficiencies in the child's learning capacity. In all that we do as educators, it is important that we focus on building upon what students already know. The more we can connect new learning to current knowledge of Black students, or any student, the more effective the teaching/learning process will be.

In seeking to provide CRP/T, we must be aware that education is, by definition, cultural. That is, our teaching always reflects

CULTURALLY RESPONSIVE PEDAGOGY/TEACHING

someone's culture; whatever we seek to teach is always accompanied by some cultural orientation. For teachers, this orientation is evidenced by the illustrations we use in the teaching/learning process: the way we dress, the pedagogical strategies and illustrations that we employ in seeking to impart the given information, our dialect, and much more. Someone's culture will always be emphasized. A fundamental key to being effective is ensuring that the learner sees *themselves* in the teaching/learning process.

Dixon (2020) reminds us that most Black schoolchildren do not have many teachers or administrators who look like them. Relatedly, they view their school climate as less positive than do their peers in other groups. For a Black child, there is value in seeing teachers and school leaders who look like them—who they can more easily relate to because of a shared cultural orientation. All else being equal, when such a connection is there, it is more likely that the teaching/learning process will be successful. The literature is replete with documentation illustrating that Black children (and all children) benefit from having educators—teachers and principals—who look like them (Lomotey & Aboh, 2015; Henderson, 2008; Kelley, 2005; Reitzug & Patterson, 1998; Tillman, 2004; Williams, 2012; Putnam, 2007).

For a teacher, being aware of the value of CRP/T is the first step in making a drastic and necessary shift in one's pedagogical approach. Here again, self-reflection is critical. A key premise is that practicing CRP/T requires a sincere desire to disrupt unethical, inequitable, and socially unjust conditions that disadvantage Blacks and other groups. This is a fundamental shift for many.

When each of these assumptions is at play, the success of the teaching/learning process is significantly more likely to come about; culture matters. Too often, we still hear so-called educators suggesting that "education is not political," or "I treat all students the same." Such views are dangerous for Black children and for all children. If a teacher treats all children the same, by definition, some children are being disenfranchised, while some children are being advantaged. In the final analysis, all children suffer. In this regard, in 2015, Aboh and I said, although educators often seek to be color-blind out of goodwill, this philosophy does not allow them to see the effect they have on students who are different. Another negative result of a presumed color-blind philosophy is the inability of educators to recognize how they render people who are different as invisible. Often educators who want to treat everyone the same, regardless of differences, treat people as if they are the same as the educator—disallowing a discussion or realization of how people do not have the same cultural norms. (p. 130)

CRP/T necessitates acknowledging and supporting the cultural differences—and similarities—that children bring to the classroom. CRP/T calls for teachers to engage in the teaching/learning process with a focus on students' strengths. Education is cultural and, as a result, it is political. As CRP/T is not always our focus as teachers, practicing and internalizing CRP/T often will necessitate a major shift in our thinking—and in our behavior.

## *CRP/T and Ethno-Humanism*

While my work on ethno-humanism has focused on Black principals, there is evidence that Black teachers also employ this role identity, as suggested by Weaver (2009). Moreover, in part because of the primary importance of the teacher in the teaching/learning process, much of the impact of the school leader is because of their interaction with—and effect upon—the teacher. Successful Black teachers, such as those described by Ladson-Billings (1994), display confidence in Black children, commitment to their education, and compassion for them, their families, and their communities.

## Culturally Responsive Pedagogy/Teaching and Ethno-Humanism

No doubt, the reader has noted in this volume—and elsewhere—the similarities between ethno-humanism and CRP/T. Table 7.1 illustrates the parallels between CRP/T and ethno-humanism. As the table illustrates, those who research and ponder the characteristics of CRP/T, include in their writings a focus on confidence, commitment, and compassion—the three C's of ethno-humanism. And their descriptions build on these three C's. Their conceptions of CRP/T also include affirming, knowing about, being concerned about, and caring about all students. They also focus on encouraging fortitude and determination in all students.

**Table 7.1.**

*Ethno-Humanism and Culturally Responsive Pedagogy/Teaching*

| Educator Characteristics | Ethno-Humanism | Culturally Responsive Pedagogy/Teaching |
|---|---|---|
| Certainty and assurance about student success | Confidence in the ability of all children to be successful (Lomotey, 1993) | Acknowledging the capacity of all students to achieve academic success (Gay, 2010; Ladson-Billings, 1994; Talbert-Johnson, 2006; Tatum, 2007) |
| Engagement with and responsibility for students | Commitment to the education of all children (Lomotey, 1993) | Teacher engagement and responsibility (Gay, 2010) |
| Empathy and kindness toward students | Compassion for all children, their families, and their communities (Lomotey, 1993) | A caring personality (Ware, 2006) |
| Engendering students' strength and confidence | ———— | Empowering of students (Ladson-Billings, 1994) |
| Acknowledging, understanding, respecting, and valuing students' cultures | Enabling students to see themselves in the curriculum (Lomotey, 1989) | Drawing on the culture of the learner, using cultural referents in instruction (Ladson-Billings, 1994; Gay, 2010; Lomotey, 1989) |

## Summary

The significance herein for Black children is threefold. First, with an added focus on these characteristics of successful principals (and teachers) there is a much better likelihood that larger numbers of Black children will be successful: academically, socially, culturally, and spiritually. Second, if we can incorporate CRP/T in classrooms across the country, Black children and all children will benefit not just because of seeing themselves in the curriculum and learning about themselves and their people; they will also be advantaged because of learning about other peoples and the relationships between their people and other peoples of the world.

Finally, a CRP/T environment will go a long way toward the elimination/eradication of institutionalized White supremacy and its devastating effect on Black people and other historically marginalized groups in the U.S.

CRP/T is necessary to facilitate the academic, social, cultural, and spiritual success of Black students and of all students. In this chapter, I have considered what CRP/T is, the assumptions related to utilizing CRP/T, the importance of CRP/T, its relationship to ethno-humanism, and its potential impact on Black children.

## Discussion Questions

1. Consider and discuss the assumptions presented in this chapter relative to effectively employing culturally responsive pedagogy/teaching. How important are these assumptions? Is this list exhaustive?

2. Consider and discuss the illustrations in this chapter of how culture is reflected in instruction. In what other ways do teachers employ a particular cultural orientation when engaging in the teaching/learning process within the classroom?

CULTURALLY RESPONSIVE PEDAGOGY/TEACHING 143

3. Consider and discuss your sense of what culturally responsive pedagogy/teaching is and its importance.

# *References*

Dixon, R. D. (2020). *A critical quantitative exploration of the state of Black education.* https://blackteachercollaborative.org/wp-content/uploads/2021/05/The-State-of-Black-Education-2021.pdf

Foster, M. (1995). *African American teachers and culturally relevant pedagogy.* ERIC, *ED38276.* https://eric.ed.gov/?id=ED382726

Gay, G. (2010). *Culturally responsive teaching: Theory, research, and practice.* Teachers College Press.

Henderson, G. (2008). *Leadership experiences of male African-American secondary urban principals: The impact of beliefs, values, and experiences on school leadership practices* [Unpublished doctoral dissertation]. Cleveland State University.

Howard, T. C. (2010). Culturally relevant pedagogy: Ingredients for critical reflection. *Theory Into Practice, 42*(3), 195–202.

Kelley, G. J. (2005). *How do principals' behaviors facilitate or inhibit the development of a culturally relevant learning community?* [Unpublished doctoral dissertation]. Indiana State University.

Ladson-Billings, G. (1994). *The dreamkeepers: Successful teachers of African American children.* John Wiley and Sons.

Lomotey, K. (1989). Culturally diversity in the urban school: Implications for principals. *NASSP Bulletin, 73*(521), 81–85.

Lomotey, K. (1993). African-American principals: Bureaucrat/administrators and ethno-humanists. *Urban Education, 27*(4), 395–412.

Lomotey, K., & Aboh, S. (2015). Urban schools, Black principals, and Black students. In M. Khalifa, N. W. Arnold, & A. F. Osanloo (Eds.), *Handbook of urban educational leadership* (pp. 118–134). Rowan & Littlefield.

Putnam, R. D. (2007). E pluribus unum: Diversity and community in the twenty-first century. The 2006 Johan Skytte Prize Lecture. *Scandinavian Political Studies, 30*(2), 137–174.

Reitzug, U. C., & Patterson, J. (1998). "I'm not going to lose you." Empowerment through caring in an urban principal's practice with students. *Urban Education, 33*(2), 150–181.

Talbert-Johnson, C. (2006). Preparing highly-qualified teacher candidates for urban schools: The importance of dispositions. *Education and Urban Society, 39*(1), 147–160.

Tatum, B. D. (2007). *Can we talk about race? And other conversations in an era of school resegregation.* Beacon Press.

Tillman, L. C. (2004). African American principals and the legacy of *Brown. Review of Research in Education, 28*(1), 101–146.

Ware, F. (2006). Warm demander pedagogy: Culturally responsive teaching that supports a culture of achievement for African American students. *Urban Education, 41*(4), 427–456.

Weaver, T. L. (2009). *Principals' attitudes toward the use of culturally relevant pedagogy and culturally responsive leadership in predominately African American schools.* [Unpublished dissertation]. Florida Atlantic University.

Williams, I. (2012). *Race and the principal pipeline: The prevalence of minority principals in light of a largely white teacher force* [Unpublished paper].

# 8.

# CULTURALLY RESPONSIVE SCHOOL LEADERSHIP

## *Introduction*

Building on previous chapters, in this chapter I briefly summarize my work on principal leadership, specifically related to ethnohumanism, the three C's. I then discuss culturally responsive school leadership, focusing on its definition, components, importance, and pillars. Finally, I consider selected implications of this discussion for professional development, principal preparation programs, and research.

Although the relationship between teacher and student is most important—this is where the rubber meets the road—there is an important role for principals in facilitating CRP/T; this role is fulfilled through what some refer to as culturally responsive school leadership or CRSL. Principals have a key role in promoting CRP/T (Marshall & Khalifa, 2018). CRSL was derived from CRP/T and builds on my earlier work and other work with Black principals; it is philosophies, practices, and policies that help to create an inclusive environment for students and families from ethnically and culturally diverse backgrounds—largely through interactions between principals and teachers, principals and students, and principals and families and other community members (Johnson, 2014).

Current and developing circumstances in schools and communities accentuate the need for principals to acknowledge and understand their role in facilitating CRP/T. Demographic, economic, and political changes place emphasis on diversity and global economy, necessitating different leadership approaches (McCray, 2011; Vargas, 2014). These circumstances combine with the reality of the disenfranchisement, opportunity gaps, and subsequent lack of success experienced by many Black children and other children.

Principals must understand the importance of race, racism, power, and diversity and acknowledge their different social identities and positionalities while conflating this knowledge with *cultural collision* and *collusion* (McCray, 2011). CRSL is critical to address the opportunity gaps, demographic shifts, and increasing diversity in communities and schools (Lopez, 2015).

## *Ethno-Humanism*

My earlier work on ethno-humanism, along with the work of others, is foundational in understanding the more recent proliferation of CRSL scholarship. More than 30 years ago, I identified two unique role identities for Black principals that I termed the bureaucrat/administrator role identity and the ethno-humanist role identity. In this volume, I focus on the second role identity—ethno-humanism—which has since been built upon by several scholars, including Tillman (2004) and Gooden (2005). This role identity encompasses: (1) a commitment by school leaders to the education of all students; (2) confidence in the ability of all children to be successful; and (3) compassion for—and understanding of—all students, for their families, and for the communities from which they come. In 1993, I said of ethno-humanism and Black principals:

> What is needed, these principals contend, is an education about one's culture, about life and about where these African American students fit in society and in the world. In essence, these leaders encourage African-American students to look at the world though an African-centered set of lenses

that provides them with vision that is more focused, has a wider periphery and more depth. (Lomotey, 1993, p. 397)

These qualities, reflective of ethno-humanism, depict what Shujaa (1993) speaks of when he describes education (versus schooling). He speaks of the culturally responsive nature of education and its relevance for each child. Ethno-humanism is very closely linked to the CRP/T employed by successful teachers and the CRSL displayed by successful principals.

Ethno-humanism reflects qualities that are needed by teachers (confidence, commitment, and compassion). In fact, Weaver (2009) stresses the significance of studying the presence of ethno-humanism in the teaching displayed by successful educators. To attract or retain teachers who (desire to) display CRP/T, principals must display characteristics of CRSL, including ethno-humanism. Research has long informed us of the potential impact of principals on the instruction of teachers (Brookover & Lezotte, 1979; Rist, 1973).

## *Understanding Culturally Responsive School Leadership*

The significance of CRSL comes about because of the impact of institutionalized White supremacy, and because, for children of any racial or cultural group to be successful, they must be able to, as I have written elsewhere (1989), *see themselves in the curriculum*; CRP/T enables this to occur.

Principals who utilize CRSL exhibit compassion, control, and commitment (Arar et al., 2018). They show care and concern for students, they maintain significant influence over the environment, and they display a sense of obligation and devotion to the success of students in their charge.

CRSL is a reconceptualization of leadership to facilitate a challenge to dominant norms—*the way we've always done things*—and to bring about more inclusive and equitable learning (Mahoney,

2017)—enabling children of all racial and cultural backgrounds to see themselves in the curriculum. For example, in Muslim schools, according to Ezzani and Brooks (2019), CRSL is manifested around inter- and intra-faith dialogue, cultural syncretism, and a focus on U.S. Muslim identity.

According to Horsford et al. (2011), CRSL has four dimensions: (1) political, (2) pedagogical, (3) personal, and (4) professional. In displaying CRSL, principals must deal with the internal politics within the institution—with staff and parents—and the external politics of the district office and the larger community—including local, state, and federal governments. Horsford et al. (2011) explored the research on CRSL with the intent of better understanding the practices of school leadership through better linking theory, research, and practice.

Madhlangobe and Gordon (2012) tell us that, for principals, CRSL is displayed on three levels: personal (self-reflection), environmental (observing what is going on), and curricular (being involved in the teaching and learning process). They go on to cite six themes of CRSL: (1) caring, (2) building relationships, (3) being persistent and persuasive, (4) being present and communicating, (5) modeling cultural responsiveness, and (6) fostering cultural responsiveness in others.

Another aspect of CRSL emphasizes that principals using this tool focus on inclusion, equity, advocacy, and social justice (Khalifa et al., 2016). Such a multipronged approach significantly increases the likelihood that the academic, social, cultural, and spiritual needs of all students are met. Lopez (2015) suggests that principals employing CRSL are critical, reflective, purposeful, and fearless. They are also judicious, assessing situations carefully. They are thoughtful, reflecting on circumstances before they act. They are decisive and courageous. They determine what needs to be done—and they do it.

The CRSL of the principal extends beyond the school building to community-based leadership: fostering cultural recognition, revitalization, and community development (Johnson, 2014). This acknowledgement is consistent with the extensive research of

Vanessa Siddle Walker. Siddle Walker has done far-reaching work on the leadership of Black principals pre-*Brown*, and the all-important link between their schools and the larger community (Siddle Walker, 2009). According to Khalifa (2013), CRSL helps to bring about strong relations with students and communities to better serve and educate them. So, then, there is an indirect role that successful Black principals play through their all-important interactions with teachers, and a more direct role reflected in their interactions with Black students, their families, and their communities.

Principals employing CRSL must be instructional leaders who ensure that teaching practices maximize the potential for all students to be successful. These principals must take time to be self-reflective and to think honestly about how they feel about education, in general, and how they feel toward all the students in their charge. Using CRSL also necessitates a focus by principals on professional responsibility to the school and the community.

## *The Importance of Culturally Responsive School Leadership*

Why is CRSL necessary? CRSL is important because principals must be committed to addressing issues of equity, ethics, and social justice in their schools, districts, and communities—and meeting the unique needs of all students in their charge (Howard et al., 2019). With CRSL, principals encourage teachers and others to be responsive to the diverse and unique needs of students (Khalifa et al., 2016). This is critically important. Presently, we are doing a gross disservice to millions of school children every day—students whose academic, social, cultural, and spiritual needs routinely go unmet.

CRP/T is important in and of itself. It enables teachers to address many of the challenges that Black children face in our schools. But school leaders must play a role. In general, we are aware of the profound effect of principals on student success (Branch et al., 2013). Principals make a positive impact on school culture, school climate, teaching efficacy, and student outcomes. Khalifa and Milner (2018) pose three critical assumptions of CRSL:

- principals must have competency in CRP/T;
- CRP/T will not be sustained in the absence of CRSL; and
- CRSL includes critical self-reflection, culturally responsive teachers, anti-oppressive school environments, and community engagement with students.

Perhaps most importantly, principals employing CRSL can encourage and inspire teachers to (continue to) practice CRP/T. Without this encouragement, CRP/T will not be sustained. The school leader's commitment and reinforcement, displayed in part by the provision of material and human resources, are critical in ensuring the persistence of CRP/T.

With CRSL, principals can meaningfully contribute to transforming schools into places where Black students and *all* students can succeed (Lopez, 2015). With CRSL, principals can help to promote equity in diverse schools (Madhlangobe & Gordon, 2012). Employing CRSL, principals can help to respond to differences that arise in diverse settings—differences founded in the unique cultural heritages and educational histories of students, faculty, families, and communities. This is particularly significant for Black children—with a long history of being negatively impacted by institutionalized White supremacy in schools and in the larger society (Taliaferro, 2011).

Khalifa et al. (2016), in an outstanding synthesis of the literature on CRSL, provide four critical pillars of CRSL: (1) critical self-reflection, (2) development of culturally responsive faculty and staff, (3) promoting culturally responsive school environment/instruction, and (4) community engagement. There is some overlap among these pillars (e.g., developing culturally responsive faculty and promoting a culturally responsive school environment), and to a large extent, they build on the components of the ethno-humanist role identity (Lomotey, 1993).

Critical self-reflection, again, is extremely important for all educators. We must constantly consider who we are, who we are teaching, how we feel about teaching, how we feel about our students, and much more. Only through such serious reflection are we able to focus our efforts effectively on the overall success of our students.

A culturally responsive faculty and staff is developed in part through the modeling of behavior by the school leader. The principal serves as a role model and facilitates children seeing themselves in the curriculum. They also model through their behavior, a commitment to the education of all children, and confidence in their ability to be successful.

A culturally responsive school environment is facilitated in part by the principal, again, providing a model and reflecting confidence and commitment. Specifically, principals contribute to this development by encouraging and supporting the development of pedagogical approaches and curricular content that focuses on—and draws upon—the culture of the student.

Community engagement is reflected in the principal's compassion for children and for the communities from which they come. They demonstrate compassion through connecting directly with students, their families, and the larger community.

## *Where Do We Go from Here?*

### Implications for Practice, Principal Preparation Programs, and Research

*Practice.* In 2015, Lowery and I identified seven ways that school leaders can encourage the practice of CRP/T by teachers. In summary, they are:

- Getting parents involved in the schooling process;
- Facilitating culturally responsive in-class and out-of-class activities;
- Meeting the needs of immigrant children;

- Being socially active;
- Caring and being culturally uplifting for all students;
- Having high expectations for all students; and
- Offering relevant professional development for teachers.

These characteristics continue to be relevant for school leaders seeking to employ CRSL within their schools.

*Principal Preparation Programs.* Efforts should be made in principal preparation programs (and in in-service professional development curricula) to encourage candidates and sitting principals to be critically self-reflective. Self-reflection is important for (aspiring) principals. By doing so early on, prospective and sitting principals can better determine if, in fact, being a principal is really what they ought to be pursuing. By being critically self-reflective, they can ascertain if they have the capacity to display: (1) confidence in the ability of all children, (2) commitment to the education of all students, and (3) compassion for students, their families, and their communities. Again, questions that are key for prospective and sitting principals, when reflecting on the teaching/learning process, include:

- How do I feel about education?
- How do I feel about diverse student populations?
- How do I feel, emotionally, entering the school in the morning?
- How do I feel, emotionally, leaving the school at the end of the day?

Increasing one's knowledge of CRSL generally leads to a deeper commitment to meeting the needs of all students. Gordon and Ronder (2016) assessed master's degree students' responses to the introduction of the concepts of CRSL into their curriculum. The students, who were in varying stages of their graduate program, developed more sophisticated notions of CRSL because of the curriculum infusion.

CULTURALLY RESPONSIVE SCHOOL LEADERSHIP    153

*Research.* Efforts should be undertaken to produce case studies of principals who display CRSL to assess their behavior and to determine if the qualities described herein are, in fact, the key qualities of these principals. We do not yet know enough about the relationship between CRSL and CRP/T and the relationship between CRSL and ethno-humanism. Moreover, we need to explore other qualities of school leaders that may contribute to our understanding of student overall success.

## *Summary*

The role of school leaders is multidimensional and critically important. For school leaders to be successful in bringing about a culturally responsive environment, they must be focused upon ensuring that there is an institutional and a community focus on equity, ethics, and social justice. Moreover, these leaders must provide the human and material resources necessary for teachers to practice CRP/T effectively and consistently.

I have noted the three key components of CRSL: (1) compassion for students, their families, and their communities (Arar et al., 2018; Madhlangobe & Gordon, 2012; Johnson, 2014; Khalifa et al., 2016); (2) commitment to the education of all students (Horsford et al., 2011; Khalifa et al., 2016; Madhlangobe & Gordon, 2012; Mahoney, 2017); and (3) self-reflection by the principal (McCray, 2011; Horsford et al., 2011; Lopez, 2015; Madhlangobe & Gordon, 2012; Khalifa et al., 2016). The first two—compassion and commitment—are consistent with my earlier work (1993) in conjunction with the ethno-humanist role identity of Black principals.

According to Johnson (2006), culturally responsive school leaders are public intellectuals, curriculum innovators, and social activists. Moreover, an analysis of leadership for social justice must take into consideration its historical, social, and political contexts (Johnson, 2006).

In this chapter, I described CRSL and provided an understanding of the connection between CRSL and ethno-humanism. Finally,

I considered some of the implications of this work for principal practice, principal professional development programs, and research. My premise, again, is that, while the relationship between teacher and student is primary, the practice of CRSL by school leaders is critically important in sustaining the CRP/T of teachers in the teaching/learning process. I emphasized this important link. Institutionalized White supremacy has a wide-ranging impact on Black people in general, and specifically on the overall educational experiences of Black children.

## *Discussion Questions*

1. Discuss the relationship between culturally responsive pedagogy/teaching (CRP/T) and culturally responsive school leadership (CRSL). Consider the importance of CRSL in sustaining CRP/T.

2. Discuss the relationship between CRSL and ethno-humanism. What are the similarities? What are the differences?

3. Consider additional implications of his work for practice, principal professional development, and research.

## *References*

Arar, K., Orucu, D., & Kucukcayir, G. (2018). Culturally relevant school leadership for Syrian refugee students in challenging circumstances. *Educational Management Administration & Leadership*, 47(6), 960–979. https://doi.org/10.1177/1741143218775430

Branch, G. F., Hanushek, E. A., & Rivkin, S. G. (2013). School leaders matter: Measuring the impact of effective principals. *Education Next*, 13(1), 62–69.

Brookover, W., & Lezotte, L. W. (1979). *Changes in school characteristics coincident with changes in student achievement* [Unpublished doctoral dissertation]. Michigan State University.

Ezzani, M., & Brooks, M. (2019). Culturally relevant leadership: Advancing critical consciousness in American Muslim students. *Educational Administration Quarterly, 55*(5), 781–811. https://doi.org/10.1177/0013161X18821358

Gooden, M. (2005). The role of an African American principal in an urban information technology high school. *Educational Administration Quarterly, 41*(4), 630–650.

Gordon, S. P., & Ronder, E. A. (2016). Perceptions of culturally responsive leadership inside and outside of a principal preparation program. *International Journal of Educational Reform, 25*(2), 125–153.

Horsford, S. D., Grosland, T., & Gunn, K. M. (2011). Pedagogy of the personal and professional: Toward a framework for culturally relevant leadership. *Journal of School Leadership, 21*(4), 582–607. https://doi.org/10.1177/105268461102100404

Howard, A., Gray, P., & Kew, K. (2019). Creating STEM momentum: Culturally relevant leadership and Hispanic girls in high school T-STEM programs in the Southwest border region. *School Leadership Review, 15*(1), 19.

Johnson, L. (2006). Making her community a better place to live: Culturally responsive urban school leadership in historical context. *Leadership and Policy in Schools, 5*(1), 19–36.

Johnson, L. (2014). Culturally responsive leadership for community empowerment. *Multicultural Education Review, 6*(2), 145–170. doi: 1080/2005615X.2014.11102915

Khalifa, M. (2013). Creating spaces for urban youth: The emergence of culturally responsive (hip-hop) school leadership and pedagogy. *Multicultural Learning and Teaching, 8*(2), 63–93. https://doi.org/10.1515/mlt-2013-0010

Khalifa, M., Gooden, M. A., & Davis, J. E. (2016). Culturally responsive school leadership: A synthesis of the literature. *Review of Educational Research, 86*(4), 1272–1311. https://doi.org/10.3102/0034654316630383

Khalifa, M., & Milner, H. R. (2018). *Culturally responsive school leadership.* Harvard Education Press.

Lomotey, K. (1989). Cultural diversity in the urban school: Implications for principals. *NASSP Bulletin, 73*(521), 81–85.

Lomotey, K. (1993). African American principals: Bureaucrat/administrators and ethno-humanists. *Urban Education, 27*(4), 395–412.

Lomotey, K., & Lowery, K. (2015). Urban schools, Black principals, and Black students: Culturally responsive education and the ethno-humanist role identity. In M. Khalifa, N. W. Arnold, A. F. Osanloo, & C. M. Grant (Eds.), *Handbook of urban educational leadership* (pp. 118–134). Rowan and Littlefield.

Lopez, A. E. (2015). Navigating cultural borders in diverse contexts: Building capacity through culturally responsive leadership and critical praxis. *Multicultural Education Review, 7*(3), 171–184. https://doi.org/10.1080/2005615X.2015.1072080

Madhlangobe, L., & Gordon, S. P. (2012). Culturally responsive leadership in a diverse school: A case study of a high school leader. *NASSP Bulletin, 96*(3), 177–202. https://doi.org/10.1177/0192636512450909

Mahoney, A. D. (2017). Being at the heart of the matter: Culturally relevant leadership learning, emotions, and storytelling. *Journal of Leadership Studies, 11*(3), 5–60. https://doi.org/10.1002/jls.21546

Marshall, S. L., & Khalifa, M. A. (2018). Humanizing school communities: Culturally responsive leadership in the shaping of curriculum and instruction. *Journal of Educational Administration, 58*(5), 533–545. https://doi.org/10.1108/JEA-01-2018-0018

McCray, C. R. (2011). Culturally relevant leadership for the enhancement of teaching and learning in urban schools. *International Handbook of Leadership for Learning, 25*, 487–501. https://link.springer.com/chapter/10.1007/978-94-007-1350-5_28

Rist, R. (1973). *The urban school: A factory of failure.* MIT Press.

Shujaa, M. J. (1993). Education and schooling: You can have one without the other. *Urban Education, 27*(4), 328–351.

Siddle Walker, V. (2009). *Hello professor: A Black principal and professional leadership in the segregated South.* University of North Carolina Press.

Taliaferro, A. (2011). Developing culturally responsive leaders through online learning and teaching approaches. *I-Manager's Journal of Educational Technology, 8*(3), 15–20. https://doi.org/10.26634/jet.8.3.1635

Tillman, L. (2004). African American principals and the legacy of *Brown. Review of Research in Education, 28*(1), 101–146.

Vargas, S. R. (2014). Culturally relevant leadership: Women of color leading from the head's office. *Independent School, 73*(4). https://eric.ed.gov/?id=EJ1048009

Weaver, T. L. (2009). *Principals' attitudes toward the use of culturally relevant pedagogy and culturally responsive leadership in predominantly African American schools* [Unpublished doctoral dissertation]. Florida Atlantic University.

# 9.

# WHAT DOES THIS ALL MEAN FOR BLACK STUDENTS (AND BLACK PEOPLE)?

## *Introduction*

In this final chapter, I begin by looking at the work on the Black principal that was published prior to 1985. Then I review my own personal development over the years, and I consider the work that I have done. I summarize that which I have shared within this book, and I project where we need to go to increase the likelihood of Black students becoming successful in large numbers as they continue to be enrolled in U.S. (public and private) schools. I highlight the continuing significance of race, racism, and institutionalized White supremacy on the heretofore unrealized success of most Black students in U.S. schools. Specifically, I discuss: (1) the development of my interest in the leadership of Black principals; (2) the impact of institutionalized White supremacy on Black education and Black people; (3) much, if not all, of what we know to date about the leadership of Black principals—particularly as it relates to their (potential) impact on the success of Black students; and (4) the implications of that knowledge.

## *The Early Research on Black Principals*

I begin by briefly looking at the studies of Black principals that appeared before my first (1985) study. The first study of Black principals that I uncovered was published by Combs (1964). As far as I

158                                    JUSTICE FOR BLACK STUDENTS

can tell, nine studies of aspects of the leadership experiences of Black principals were conducted prior to my 1985 study. I caution the reader here in that—though the principals in the Combs and the Funches (1965) studies were principals of "secondary schools for Negroes"—nowhere in either article is the race of the principals mentioned. I assume, given the time period, that all the principals are Black.

Most of these studies explore aspects of the altered circumstances and experiences of Black principals in the South post-*Brown*. For the most part, they do not focus on the impact of the leadership of these principals on Black student success. Combs (1964) conducted a study of 115 principals in Florida. The author was exploring the work routines of these principals in predominantly Black high schools. Funches (1965) conducted a study of the work habits of 121 principals in Black high schools in Mississippi relative to the expectations of their superintendents.

Ray Rist (1972) conducted a case study of an all-Black K–8 school. This was a part of a three-year longitudinal study in which Rist was exploring the impact of the principal on the culture of the school, specifically as it impacts student success. All the students, staff, teachers, and administrators in this school were Black. This was the earliest study that I uncovered that looked specifically at the impact of Black principals on the academic success of Black students.

Chapman (1973), using survey data and school records from 1954 through 1972, explored the role expectations of Black principals as perceived by the principals themselves and by other Blacks (educators and non-educators). Everett E. Abney (1974, 1980), the area superintendent of the Dade County Public Schools in Florida, published two articles in *The Journal of Negro Education* in which he explores the treatment and displacement of Black principals in Florida post-*Brown*.

Buxton and Prichard (1977) published a study in the journal *Integrated Education,* in which they explore the self-perceptions of Black principals post-*Brown* and their perceptions of the impact of *Brown* on their schools.

WHAT DOES THIS ALL MEAN FOR BLACK STUDENTS?

Another study (1977) was conducted in Florida in which the author, S.O. Johnson, explores how Black administrators perceived the role that Black principals served in the state of Florida post-*Brown*. Lastly, Hines and Byrne (1980) published an article in which they explore Black principals' personal characteristics, working conditions, and their views on aspects of the educational experience.

In summary of these pre-1985 publications, these are very interesting studies with interesting foci. They generally focus on how these leaders' experiences and conditions changed following *Brown*. For example, they look at changes in these leaders' (1) work routines and (2) role expectations. They also explore principals' (1) self-perception of the impact of *Brown*, and (2) how they (the Black principals) were treated in the face of *Brown*. The one exception is the Rist (1972) longitudinal study—that does look at the impact of principal leadership on student academic success.

## *Autobiographical Sketch Revisited*

Shortly after I arrived in Oberlin to pursue my undergraduate degree, I began to gain greater insights into the fact that, not only did Black students have fundamentally different experiences in K–12 institutions, but they also typically had awful encounters and dreadful outcomes. While my initial interest in the miseducation of Black children started in 1970—not too long after I enrolled in Oberlin—my first response to this quagmire was not to become involved in studying the significance of the leadership of Black principals.

Within a few years after arriving at Oberlin, I became aware of independent African-centered schools, primarily on the east coast and in the Midwest, and I also learned about the Council of Independent Black Institutions, or CIBI, an umbrella organization for these schools, founded in 1972 (Lomotey, 2015). I thought about starting an independent African-centered school in Oberlin. I spoke with Omowale Babalawo, also known as Frank Satterwhite, who was an associate dean at Oberlin. Omowale had been a founding member of CIBI, having been involved with independent African-centered schools in the San Francisco Bay area. Omowale suggested that I connect with Kasisi Jitu Weusi, who was the headmaster at Uhuru Sasa Shule—Kiswahili for Freedom Now School—an independent African-centered school in Brooklyn. Jitu was also the national chair of CIBI.

I contacted Jitu and he invited me to visit Uhuru Sasa. I went to Brooklyn and spent two days with Jitu. After my visit to Uhuru Sasa, I decided to start an independent African-centered school in Oberlin—Shule ya Kujitambua—the School for Black Re-Identification, in Kiswahili.

## *My Stanford Experience*

Remember that my initial interest in the leadership of Black principals—some 40 or more years ago—grew out of my interest in improving the success and life chances of Black children—and Black people. I believed at that time (and I now know) that the presence of Black school leaders makes a positive impact on the opportunities for the success of Black students. I wanted to know what Black principals do to positively impact the success of Black students.

When I went to Stanford to work on my doctoral degree in educational leadership, I had the experience leading the Shule and I had also had numerous student leadership experiences while at Oberlin (see Introduction); leadership intrigued me, and I believed that leaders could make a difference for Black children—Black boys and Black girls.

In my first few years at Stanford, studying with Larry Cuban, Michael Kirst, and the late Ed Bridges, I noticed that all the studies that had been done on successful principals had been done with White male samples. I began to wonder if, in fact, Black principals who were successful with Black students displayed the same qualities as successful White male principals. I also wondered if there were other qualities that successful Black principals shared with each other.

As I finished my doctoral research, I had concluded that successful Black principals did, indeed, at times, display the four qualities that had been thrust upon them by earlier researchers (i.e., goal development, energy harnessing, communication facilitation, and instructional leadership). I also concluded that successful Black principals displayed what I call the three C's, or ethno-humanism—commitment, confidence, and compassion: commitment to the education of all children, confidence in the ability of all children to be successful, and compassion for all children, their families, and their communities.

I conducted additional research in which I sought to support the idea that successful principals utilized these two role identities. I branded the first set of qualities as the *bureaucrat/administrator role identity*. The three C's I branded as the *ethno-humanist role identity* (Lomotey, 1993, 1994).

I continued to explore the Black principalship after leaving Stanford. My colleague, Kendra Lowery, and I reviewed 31 research studies on the leadership of successful Black principals and argued that these leaders contribute to increased Black student success by providing a culturally responsive educational experience/culturally responsive leadership (Lomotey & Lowery, 2014). This review focused on studies published between 1987 and 2012. More recently, I reviewed 57 studies of Black women principals (Lomotey, 2019). These were studies of Black women principals (in the U.S.) published between 1993 and 2017. In this book, I report for the first time on my study of Black male principals as reflected in 29 studies of these leaders that appeared between 1975 and 2021 (Chapter 5 in this volume). Much of this more recent work draws on related work that had been done by others in the interim—scholars such as my good friends, Linda Tillman (2004) and Mark Gooden (2005).

## *Institutionalized White Supremacy*

We live in a society where Black people continue to be oppressed and powerless in the face of persistent institutionalized White supremacy. While I acknowledge that institutionalized White supremacy impacts Latinx, Asian American, and Indigenous Peoples to varying degrees, and while I am aware of other forms of devastating oppression that impact people based on their class, gender, sexual orientation, religion (or lack thereof), age, height, weight, "beauty," abledness, and more, my focus in this book—and indeed in the bulk of my scholarly work—is on the experiences of people of African descent: Black people.

Institutionalized White supremacy has a long excruciating history in the U.S. and beyond and remains painfully impactful today. Most notably, for our purposes, it continues to negatively affect the experiences of Black students in U.S. education. As we proceed through the third decade of the $21^{st}$ century, one of the most—if not *the* most—significant factor negatively impacting the life chances of Black people in the U.S. continues to be institutionalized White supremacy (Shockley & Lomotey, 2020).

*I do not believe that U.S. public schools will ever meet the academic, social, cultural, and spiritual needs of the masses of Black children.* What is institutionalized White supremacy? It is, in part, the belief in the inferiority of Black people *coupled with* the exercise of power and privilege over them. Recall that Wade Nobles (1978) defines power as the ability to explain reality and to convince others that it is *their* reality—*their* worldview.

Jake Carruthers (1995) describes the idea of a worldview. He says, "worldview . . . includes the way a people conceive of the fundamental questions of existence and organization of the universe" (p. 53). Lomotey and Aboh (2009) expand this discussion of a worldview, as it relates to Black people:

> It is, in a sense, the lens through which one views the world. Too often, students of African descent in the United States

# WHAT DOES THIS ALL MEAN FOR BLACK STUDENTS? 163

> receive an educational experience from a European world-view perspective that does not instill in them any desire to develop the communities populated by people of African descent. (p. 315)

What does this have to do with the leadership of Black principals and the academic, social, cultural, and spiritual success of Black children? Institutions, by definition, are subjective; they are more often designed to seamlessly produce people and systems to further the status quo.

Recall the bureaucrat/administrator role identity. This role identity is significantly more prominent in U.S. schools than is the ethno-humanist role identity. Indeed, the structured evaluations and assessments of school leaders focus nearly exclusively on aspects of this role identity. Schools are intended, in most instances, to maintain the status quo; the bureaucrat/administrator role identity reinforces this mission. Maintenance of the status quo ensures that the existing power relations are maintained.

Shujaa's (1993) teachings, again, are instructive here. In distinguishing schooling from education, he reminded us that:

> Schooling is a process intended to perpetuate and maintain society's existing power relations and the institutional structures that support those arrangements. . . . Education in contrast to schooling is our means of providing for intergenerational transmission of cultural identity through knowledge of the values, beliefs, traditions, customs, rituals, and sensibilities that have sustained a people. (p. 15)

Schooling extends prevailing power relationships and perpetuates the existing politically controlling cultural orientation. It occurs when one group has power over another. Through schooling, the culture of a dominant group is imposed upon others. The group that is imposed upon adjusts and adapts in response to contact with the dominant—and privileged—group (Shujaa, 1993).

On the other hand, education is learning and internalizing one's own cultural norms. It occurs in informal and formal settings. It provides the wherewithal for members of a group to effectively function within their family, community, and race and to retain the integrity of their own culture in social contexts where unequal power relations exist among cultures (Shujaa, 1993).

We are all being schooled, because of institutionalized White supremacy, White privilege, and the power that White people hold over other groups in society. In addition, Black people in the U.S.—and elsewhere—receive much less education because of the power exerted by Whites. Because of the power relations that exist in the U.S., Black people experience significantly more schooling than education (Shujaa, 1993).

The curriculum in U.S. public schools does not encourage Black students:

- to learn to think critically,
- to learn and know about themselves,
- to learn the cultures and stories of Black people,
- to learn to appreciate different worldviews, or
- to learn to work toward self-actualization.

## *Summary*

In contextualizing my thinking on the education of Black people, in the Introduction, I set the tone for subsequent discussions about my personal development, why I pursued the line of research that I pursued, and why I have consistently focused on strategies that are intended to improve the success of Black children—and, ultimately, all children. It is important, I believe, to understand the historical practices in U.S. education that have impacted the life chances of Black children—the theories used to explain most circumstances. Importantly, in the Introduction, I lay out the impact of institutionalized White supremacy on the education of Black children. In the Introduction, I also introduce a discussion to which I return several times—the distinction between schooling and education (Shujaa, 1993) and the impact of each on Black children.

My autobiographical discussion, primarily in Chapter 1 and reprised earlier in this chapter, provides a snapshot of the experiences and encounters that helped to shape my thinking and, more importantly, to develop my commitment to Black education and to improving the overall experiences of Black children. Such a context is important, I believe, in contextualizing and explaining my current thinking and my subsequent work.

My initial research on Black principal leadership took place beginning in 1985. In Chapter 2, I provide a reprint of my 1987 article that summarizes that initial research on Black principals. The article describes my interest in two key research questions.

In 1993, I coined the terms ethno-humanism and bureaucrat/administrator to describe the two role identities that I had identified earlier. My 1993 article, reprinted as Chapter 3, introduces those two role identities through a study of two Black principals. In this reprinted article, I make the important link between my work on those two role identities and the work of Shujaa (1993) on schooling and education.

In 2019, I published an article on Black women principals, summarizing the work that had been done to date on these leaders. In Chapter 4, I reprint that article, while noting that significant additional work has been done in this area since the publication of that article. I emphasize that significantly more work needs to be done on these important leaders.

In Chapter 5, I present a new study of Black male principals. There is more research needed on Black male principals and Black women principals. I emphasize this point after conducting this literature review on studies of Black male principals.

My work over the years has been focused largely on a discussion of the three C's: ethno-humanism. This is the case because I believe—and my research supports the idea—that this role identity is key in terms of characteristics that are critical for Black school leaders who are committed to the success of Black students. In Chapter 6, I offer an extended discussion of this role identity focused on my own work, and on the work of others in this area.

In acknowledging the fundamental role of CRP/T and the relationship between the teacher and the student, I focus on CRP/T in Chapter 7. Therein, I discuss the relevance of CRP/T for Black children and consider the all-important relationship between CRP/T and ethno-humanism, and the benefits of both for Black children. In this chapter, I highlight six important assumptions related to CRP/T that every educator (and parent and community member) should be cognizant of as they seek to contribute to the overall success of Black children. In addition, I focus, in the chapter, on the importance of eliminating institutionalized White supremacy and its relationship to Black student success.

I have argued herein that the most important relationship within the school is that which exists between the teacher and the student; this relationship is paramount. I also believe that the role of the principal in bringing about a school-wide focus on CRP/T—through CRSL—is tremendous. In Chapter 8, I discuss the significance of CRSL for Black children. I talk in Chapter 8 about implications of the importance of CRSL for practice, principal preparation, and research.

## *Implications*

Generally, the more we learn about the leadership characteristics of Black principals, the more we can understand what contributes to greater success for Black students. The more we learn about ethno-humanism, the better equipped we are to address the success of Black students. While I have highlighted the limited work that occurred pre-1985—largely to document this important history—we know that the overwhelming majority of research on Black principals occurred in the past 40 years.

## Practice Implications

In 2015, Lomotey and Lowery put forth five recommendations for the practice of Black principals. They are:

- Guide teachers in providing CRP/T;

- Stress the importance of education with students;

- Foster meaningful relationships with the community surrounding the school;

- Embrace a caring and nurturing disposition; and

- Emphasize the centrality of intercultural understanding, appreciation, and respect.

These recommendations continue to be pregnant with relevance.

## Research Implications

This discussion presented within these pages provides a tremendous amount of information that could lead to theory-testing research and additional practitioner-oriented research as well as qualitative research, including extensive action research. Some queries of continuing relevance were put forth by Lomotey and Lowery (2015). They include:

- How do successful Black principals focus on student needs?

- In what ways do successful Black principals guide teachers in providing a CRP/T?

- How do successful Black principals stress education with their students?

- How do successful Black principals display confidence in the ability of all students to be successful?

- How do successful Black principals work with communities to improve schools?

- What are the characteristics of successful Black principals who show a nurturing/caring disposition?
- To what extent do successful Black teachers display ethno-humanism?

On the tertiary level, we need more research on historically Black colleges and universities (HBCUs). HBCUs continue to produce more Black doctors, engineers, lawyers, judges, and graduates in other high-profile professions. Twenty-five percent of Black college graduates in STEM fields graduate from HBCUs. In addition, the six-year graduation rate for Black students at HBCUs exceeds that of Black graduates of predominantly White colleges and universities (Dixon, 2020). These data should be studied. If Black college students are achieving greater levels of success in institutions with large numbers of Black faculty and administrators (i.e., HBCUs), there is likely data there that could be instructive in our efforts to improve the overall success of Black pre-collegiate students.

Other relevant—but currently underexplored—research questions derived from this work include:

- Are there differences in the leadership of Black male principals and Black women principals?
- What aspects of the leadership of Black principals pre-*Brown* are instructive in terms of the current needs of Black children?
- What barriers, if any, detract from the ability of Black principals to display CRSL? How might these barriers be addressed?
- What other strategies, aside from CRSL, may be of value in addressing the overall success of Black students (e.g., independent African-centered schools, or, at least, some of the strategies employed in these schools)?
- To what extent are principal preparation programs (PPPs) preparing prospective school leaders to employ CRSL?

WHAT DOES THIS ALL MEAN FOR BLACK STUDENTS? 169

What efforts might assist in increasing the emphasis on CRSL within PPPs?

## *Final Thoughts*

The importance of additional explorations of the overall success of Black children and the leadership of Black principals cannot be overstated. The miseducation of Black children continues to be in a crisis state. This will be the case as long as institutionalized White supremacy continues to raise its ugly head in U.S. education and in other institutions throughout this country. As Dixon (2020) advises:

> Research on Black students should therefore be intentional about understanding the communities' histories, current contexts, and what their future might look like. If not, reform efforts will continue to lack relevance for Black people and fail to create more opportunities for success. (p.7)

It is not an accident, nor should it be a surprise, that the reader would be challenged to identify *one* reform effort that has been put in place in U.S. schools—since it became legal to educate Black children—that has benefitted the masses of Black children; there are none. They are not designed to do that.

This is not an issue of "fixing Black children." As Dixon (2020) says: "We need to fix the system and policies that consistently hinder Black children from experiencing a positive educational environment" (p. 14). The challenge is systemic issues—embodied in institutionalized White supremacy—that negatively influence the road to success for these children.

Still, I believe that work being done on equity audits, extending the school day, extending the school year, infusing Black Studies in the curriculum, equalizing expenditures in school districts, seeking to employ culturally responsive pedagogy, desegregating schools, establishing charter schools, and many of the other myriad reform efforts, all have the *potential* to bring about improvements in the life chances of Black children. I believe that the work of many scholars can also have an impact on the academic, social, cultural, and spiritual success of Black children. Ron Edmonds put it best 40 years ago (1979), when he said:

> It seems to me, therefore, that what is left of this discussion are three declarative statements: (a) We can, whenever and wherever we choose, successfully teach all children whose schooling is of interest to us; (b) We already know more than we need to do that; and (c) Whether or not we do it must finally depend on how we feel about the fact that we haven't so far. (p. 23)

Finally, I believe that my work—and the work of others—on Black principals is important also because it, too, will have an impact on some leaders and, subsequently, on some Black children. I, along with others, have demonstrated that Black principals make a difference for Black students. When Black principals display ethno-humanism, it serves our students well.

I unambiguously understand that the relationship between teachers and students is the most important bond in schools; this is where *the rubber meets the road*. But, in addition, as school leaders, the role of Black principals is critical; without them displaying ethno-humanism and CRSL, the teaching of CRP/T will not be sustained. As Frederick Douglass told us: "Power concedes nothing without a demand. It never did and it never will." And so, the work continues.

## *Discussion Questions*

1. Consider and discuss where research now needs to focus to address Black student academic, social, cultural, and spiritual success.

2. Consider what can be done to address the negative impact of institutionalized White supremacy on the overall success of Black students.

## *References*

Abney, E. E. (1974). The status of Florida's Black school principals. *The Journal of Negro Education, 43*(1), 3–8.

Abney, E. E. (1980). A comparison of the status of Florida's Black public school principals, 1964–65/1975–76. *The Journal of Negro Education, 49*(4), 398–406.

Buxton, H., & Prichard, K. (1977). The power erosion syndrome of the Black principal. *Integrated Education, 3*(15), 9–14.

Carruthers, J. (1995). Black intellectuals and the crisis in Black education. In M. J. Shujaa (Ed.), *Too much schooling, too little education: A paradox of Black life in White societies* (pp. 35–55). Africa World Press.

Chapman, R. L. (1973). *The role expectation of the Black urban principal as perceived by himself, administrators, influentials, and other active community persons* [Paper presentation]. The annual meeting of the American Educational Research Association, New Orleans, LA.

Combs, W. E. (1964). The principalship in Negro secondary schools of Florida. *The Bulletin of the National Association of Secondary School Principals, 48*(293), 14–22.

Dixon, R. D. (2020). *A critical quantitative exploration of the state of Black education.* https://blackteachercollaborative.org/wp-content/uploads/2021/05/The-State-of-Black-Education-2021.pdf

Edmonds, R. (1979). Effective schools for the urban poor. *Educational Leadership, 37*(1), 15–24.

Funches, D. (1965). The superintendent's expectations of the Negro high school principal in Mississippi. *Journal of Experimental Education, 34*(1), 73–77.

Gooden, M. (2005). The role of an African American principal in an urban information technology high school. *Educational Administration Quarterly, 41*(4), 630–650.

Hines, S. A., & Byrne, D. R. (1980). In portrait: Black principals: NASSP study provides meaningful data. *NASSP Bulletin, 64*(433), 767–776.

Johnson, S. O. (1977). A study of the perceptions of Black administrators concerning the role of the Black principal in Florida during the period 1973–78. *The Journal of Negro Education, 46*(1), 53–61.

Lomotey, K. (1985). Black Principals in Black Elementary Schools: School Leadership and School Success. [Unpublished doctoral dissertation]. Stanford University.

Lomotey, K. (1987). Black principals for Black students: Some preliminary observations. *Urban Education, 22*(2), 173–181.

Lomotey, K. (1990). Qualities shared by African-American principals in effective schools: A preliminary analysis. In K. Lomotey (Ed.), *Going to school: The African-American experience* (pp. 180–195). SUNY Press.

Lomotey, K. (1993). African American principals: Bureaucrat/administrators and ethno-humanists. *Urban Education, 27*(4), 395–412.

Lomotey, K. (1994). African-American principals: Bureaucrat/administrators and ethno-humanists. In M. J. Shujaa (Ed.), *Too much schooling, too little education: A paradox of Black life in White societies* (pp. 203-220). Africa World Press.

Lomotey, K. (2015). Council of Independent Black Institutions. In M. J. Shujaa & K. J. Shujaa (Eds.), *The SAGE encyclopedia of African cultural heritage in North America* (pp. 300–308). SAGE.

Lomotey, K. (2019). Research on the leadership of Black women principals: Implications for Black students. *Educational Researcher, 48*(6), 336–348.

Lomotey, K., & Aboh, S. (2009). Historically Black colleges and universities: Catalysts to liberation? In L. C. Tillman (Ed.), *The SAGE Handbook of African American education* (pp. 311–318). SAGE Publications.

Lomotey, K., & Lowery, K. (2014). Black students, urban schools and Black principals: Leadership practices that address disenfranchisement. In H. R. Milner & K. Lomotey (Eds.), *Handbook of urban education* (pp. 325–349). Routledge.

Lomotey, K., & Lowery, K. (2015). Urban schools, Black principals and Black students: Culturally responsive education and the ethno-humanist role identity. In M. Khalifa, C. Grant, & N. Witherspoon Arnold (Eds.), *Urban school leadership handbook* (pp. 118–134). Rowman & Littlefield.

Nobles, W. (1978). *African consciousness and liberation struggles: Implications for the development and construction of scientific paradigms* [Unpublished paper].

Rist, R. C. (1972). *On the role of principal as "cultural maximizer" in an urban Black school* (ED 073-206). ERIC.

Shockley, K., & Lomotey, K. (2020). Introduction. In K. Shockley & K. Lomotey (Eds.) *African-centered education: Theory and practice.* Myers Education Press.

Shujaa, M. J. (1993). Education and schooling: You can have one without the other. *Urban Education, 27*(4), 328–351.

Tillman, L. C. (2004). African American principals and the legacy of *Brown. Review of Research in Education, 28,* 101–146.

# AFTERWORD

*"And how are the children?"*
*(African greeting)*

This book, *Justice for Black Students: Black Principals Matter*, is a very important contribution to the literature on Blacks in the principalship. This book is also very important for today's conversations about principal leadership and the education of Black children. It would have also been very important in the pre-*Brown* era of education when Black children were mostly taught and led by Black educators. It would have also been very important in the immediate post-*Brown* era of education when, after the firing and demotion of thousands of Black educators, Black children had little contact with Black educators and, in some cases, were denied their right to attend school due to the closing of many schools after the *Brown* decision. The topic of Black principal leadership is timeless in terms of its importance to the lives of Black children and Black people.

As Dr. Lomotey has correctly noted, prior to his early work on Black principal leadership, the literature on this topic was almost non-existent. Today, while there is much more research and scholarship on this topic, the U.S. education system is still very much in need of a critique with respect to its treatment of Black children. We need a critique of the kind of principal leadership Black children need—what kind of principal leadership will help them to expect and experience success and receive a quality education.

Data from the National Center for Education Statistics (NCES) indicate that for the 2017–2018 school year (the last year for which data are available), 15.1% of all students in public schools were Black. Yet only 10.7% of all principals and 7.0% of all teachers nationwide were Black (NCES, 2020). Clearly, there is a very weak pipeline with respect to Black principals and teachers—educators who are needed to provide Black children with the social, emotional, and academic nurturing and care they need.

Dr. Lomotey describes a *quality education* as one wherein students are academically, socially, culturally, and spiritually successful. In his discussion of what a quality education means for Black children, he asks a thought-provoking question: "Who can provide this type of education for Black children?" Dr. Lomotey points to the leadership of Black principals as not only an answer to this question, but an imperative. Black children can and do benefit from the leadership of Black principals—leadership that is attuned to the unique cultural needs of Black children.

While the importance of Black principals in the education and lives of Black children has been of extreme importance since the pre-*Brown* era of education, it is especially important today. Today, Black children are subjected to persistent racism, lack of resources, and academic underachievement. For example, the standardized test scores of Black children continue to lag behind their White and Asian counterparts. Data from the 2017 National Center for Education Statistics indicate that Black children scored below average on the National Assessment of Education Progress 4th, 8th, and 12th grade reading and math tests (NCES, 2020). Thus, in 2022, we continue to be faced with a crisis in terms of the achievement and opportunity gaps that are prevalent in the lives of Black children, in both schools and society.

When we think about ways to address and close these gaps, and the type of principal leadership that will lead to a quality education for Black children, there is another very important question that also must be addressed: What are we willing to do to ensure that Black children receive a quality education? That is, how will we get justice for Black children? How will we ensure that Black children experience success, not just based on standardized test scores, but based on a more holistic model of education that focuses on the academic, social, cultural, and spiritual growth of Black children?

AFTERWORD 177

How can Black principal leadership be a key factor in the success of these children?

Several prominent themes in this book address the importance of Black principal leadership and a quality education for Black children.

## A Black Principal Pipeline

There is an imperative and an urgency to increase the pipeline of Black principals. There has been no consistent increase in the numbers of Black women and men who lead K–12 schools. Yet, research by Dr. Lomotey and others provides examples of the positive influences that Black principals can have in the lives of Black children. A shared culture with Black principals can lead to higher rates of student achievement and success and address both the achievement and opportunity gaps that exist for Black students. Further, Black principals can instill a sense of belonging in Black children; that is, seeing and interacting with Black principals can lead Black children to believe that they can succeed. The cultural nurturing, encouragement, and care that Black principals can provide to Black children speaks to the urgency to increase the numbers of Black men and women who become principals. More Black principals are also needed so that their numbers reflect the demographics of Black children in schools today and in the future. Black children benefit from seeing and interacting with leaders who look like them.

## Ethno-Humanist Principal Preparation

There is an imperative and urgency to promote and widely adopt principal preparation models that include the ethno-humanist model of school leadership. Principal preparation programs should be structured so that there is an emphasis on how to successfully merge culturally responsive school leadership models that focus on equity, ethics, social justice, and the elimination of institutional White supremacy, with ethno-humanist leadership practices that focus on confidence, commitment, and compassion. Many Black principal candidates will lead schools in districts that have single-race schools and serve poor and low-income Black children. These candidates must be trained to work with teachers, students, parents, and other school personnel by using practices that are attentive to the racial and cultural norms of Black people. The content of the principal preparation programs should be intentional and should include reflective practices that give teachers and other school personnel opportunities to think critically about their teaching and other interactions with Black children. Principals must also help teachers and other school personnel to understand how Black children's experiences in education and society can impact their classroom experiences and their perspectives on the value of education.

## *Education or Schooling*

There is an imperative and an urgency to prepare teachers and principals to adopt a philosophy and pedagogy wherein education is valued over schooling. That is, principals must not only assist teachers in becoming proficient in culturally responsive pedagogy, but also help them to understand why culturally responsive pedagogy is critical to Black student success. Both principals and teachers must understand that it is necessary to adopt practices that do more than replicate the status quo of education (schooling). Principals must focus on the education of Black students by adopting a curriculum that addresses the cultures of Black students, allows them to see themselves in the curriculum, and bridges the connection between culturally responsive pedagogy and ethno-humanism. Principals must be proactive in making sure that teachers consistently consider issues of race and culture in their pedagogical practice, and that they reflect on their classroom practices and their interactions with Black students.

# AFTERWORD

Dr. Lomotey states, "I do not believe that U.S. public schools will ever meet the academic, social, cultural, and spiritual needs of the masses of Black children." He explains that his pessimism is due to the institutionalized White supremacy that has negatively impacted the life chances of Black people. Additionally, he points out that because of White supremacy, many Black children rarely receive a quality education; rather, they are socialized to accept a type of *schooling* that perpetuates a status quo where Black children are often subjected to inequitable teaching and leadership. He also points out that the "historical practices in U.S. education" have continued to place Black children in a subordinate position.

Given Dr. Lomotey's observations, we too might be pessimistic about the future of our Black children. However, we must consider the positive impact that Black principals can have in the lives of Black children. Black principals can work to get justice for Black children. Black principals can be the catalyst that education and society need to reverse the persistence of the under-education of Black children. I am hopeful that the pipeline of Black principals will increase. I am hopeful that the wisdom, knowledge, care, and nurturing by Black principals will make a difference in the lives of current and future generations of Black children who are often viewed as "somebody else's problem." I am hopeful that in the not-too-distant future we can ask the question often heard in an African greeting: "And how are the children?" and our response will be "All the children are well."

*Linda C. Tillman, PhD*
*Professor Emerita, University of North Carolina, Chapel Hill*

## *Reference*

National Center for Education Statistics. (2020). *Digest of education statistics.* https://nces.ed.gov/programs/digest/

# ABOUT THE AUTHOR

For a half-century, **KOFI LOMOTEY** has been concerned about the limited academic, social, cultural, and spiritual success of children of African ancestry in U.S. schools. Virtually all of his research, publishing, experience in the academy, and practice have focused in one way or another on this longstanding crisis. As a researcher, his work has focused largely on the significance of Black principals for the overall success of Black children. He has published more than 50 books, journal articles, and book chapters, with most focused on aspects of Black education—from pre-K to professional school. His publications include: (1) the 1,100-page *Encyclopedia of African American Education* (SAGE, 2010); (2) "Research on the Leadership of Black Women Principals: Implications for Black Children" (*Educational Researcher*, 2019); and (3) *African-Centered Education: Theory and Practice* (co-edited with Kmt G. Shockley, Myers Education Press, 2020).

As an academic, Kofi has been a professor, a department chair, a provost (twice), and a campus CEO (twice). As a practitioner, he has helped to establish and led three independent African-centered schools. Currently, he is the Chancellor John Bardo and Deborah Bardo Distinguished Professor of Educational Leadership at Western Carolina University. In 2020, he received the Roald F. Campbell Award from the University Council for Educational Administration, an annual award that recognizes a senior professor of educational leadership for a lifetime of excellent achievement. In 2021, Kofi was elected as a Fellow of the American Educational Research Association.

Kofi has been married to A. Nahuja since 1977. They have a daughter (Shawnjua Tien), two sons (Juba Jabulani and Mbeja Makiri), and five grandchildren (Ayanna, Isaiah Jelani, Nia Marie, Norah Sanaa, and Zola Therese).

# INDEX

## A

Abney, E.E., 158
Aboh, S., xvii, 139, 162
Adkins-Sharif, J., 102
Adkison, J.A., 76
Adult Development Theory, 101, 105
African American Community and Student
    Development Program (AACSDP), 6
African American Male, 101
Afrikan Heritage House, 8
Akbar, N., 10
All-African People's Revolutionary Party
    (AAPRP), 9
Allen, K., 76
Alston, K.R., 108
Anderson, R., 106
anti-Blackness, 102
Arar, K., 147, 153
Armstrong, D., 62
Arnold, N.W., 62

## B

Babalawo, O., 4, 9, 6–7, 159–60
Bagwell, C.L., 60
Banks, E.M., 97, 104
Beachum, F., xxiv
Bell, D.A., 69, 99
Best, M.L., 62
Bethune, M.M., 56, 96
Black children
    defining quality education for, xix
    holistic education of, 176
    inequality of, xvi
    opportunity gap and, xvi
    perception of having something
    wrong with them, xvi
    test scores and, 176
black cultural views, 18
Black English, 138
Black Feminist Standpoint Theory (BFST), 69
Black Feminist Thought (BFT), 57, 64, 66, 68,
    69, 70, 74, 75, 77

Black male principals, research on, 95, 108–9,
    111–12
    background of research, 95–97
    benefit to Black students, 106
    bureaucrat/administrator role iden-
    tity of, 107
    career aspirations of, 104–8
    case studies about, 107
    commitment to students, 105–6
    ethno-humanist role identities of,
    107, 109
    findings of research, 98–101
    five key leadership components of,
    128
    implications of research, 109–11
    increasing number of Black female
    principals, 96–97
    list of studies reviewed, 117–19
    nature of research about, 102–8
    predominance in educational insti-
    tutions, 96
    principal characteristics of, 106–7
    research methods, 97–98
    success stories about, 107–8
    three qualities shared by (3 Cs),
    xxi, xxii, xxiii, xxiv, 32, 44–45, 123–
    26, 128–29, 130, 131, 145, 147, 153, 161,
    165–66
    underrepresentation of, 108
Black Masculine Caring, 101
Black principal pipeline, 176
Black principals, 157
    as bureaucrat/administrators, xii–xiii,
    xxiii, xxvi, 29–30, 33, 35–43, 146, 161
    common characteristics of, 16
    community involvement and, 21, 22
    compassion and, 22
    culture and, 17
    early research about, 157–59
    effective communication with Black
    students, 19
    embracing Black culture, xx

183

ethno-humanist role identity, xii–
xiii, xxi, xxiii, xxiv, 29–30, 33, 44–47,
130, 146–47, 161
female, xxiii–xxiv
four qualities of in effective schools,
32, 161
homophily and, 19, 20, 33
implications of research about,
166–68
as members of cultural groups, 48
three qualities shared by (3 Cs),
xxi, xxii, xxiii, xxiv, 16, 32, 44–45,
123–26, 128–29, 130, 131, 145, 147, 153,
161, 165–66
Black School Principal Changed My Life, A,
125
Black students, 162–64, 164–66, 169–70
academic disenfranchisement of, 31
academic success of, xv, 58, 95
disenfranchisement of, 57–58
overall success of, xv
performance in Oberlin schools, 5
teacher race and, 20–21
teacher/student relationships and, 58
theories for lack of success of,
xvi–xvii
Black Studies curriculum, 169–70
Black, W.J., 104
Black women principals, research on, 57–58,
60–61
academic preparation of, 91
age range of, 90
bibliographies of studies on, 85–90
dearth of research about, 60
dissertation research on, 71
frameworks of research about, 64,
74–75
impact on inner-city schools, 64
levels of leadership and, 65
levels of schools researched, 70–71,
92
major findings in research about,
65–66
mentoring and, 76
method of research on, 61–63, 72–73,
91
number of studies devoted to, 91
oppression of, 59, 73–74
principal preparation and, 76
principal professional development
and, 76
purpose of researching, 59–60

research methods, 64–65
six research questions about, 61
spirituality and, 64, 66–68, 76, 92
statistics about, 58, 62–63
tenure in U.S. schools, 90
theoretical frameworks of research,
68–70
three qualities shared by (3 Cs),
xxi, xxii, xxiii, xxiv, 32, 44–45, 123–
26, 128–29, 130, 131, 145, 147, 153, 161,
165–66
types of studies about, 63
urbanicity and, 68
Blauner, R., 17
Bloom, C.M., xxiii, 68
*Boston Globe*, 125
Bowles, S., xvi, 32
Branch, G.F., 149
Bridges, E., 12, 98, 160
Bronx High School of Science, 3
Brookins, C., 43
Brooklyn Technical High School, 3
Brookover, W., 15, 16, 42, 147
Brooks, A.E., xxiv, 102, 105, 107
Brooks, J.S., 62
Brooks, M., 148
Brown, C.A., 71
*Brown v. Board of Education*, 56, 96, 128
Buffalo Public Schools, 34
bureaucratic/administrator role identity,
xii–xiii, xxiv, xxvi, 29–30, 35–43, 161,
163, 165
Black male principals and, 107
communication facilitation and,
40–42
curriculum planning and, 42–43
energy harnessing and, 37–39
ethno-humanism and, 127, 129
goal development and, 35–36
instructional management and,
42–43
teacher supervision and, 43
Buxton, H., 158
Byrne, D.R., 159

## C

California State Department of Education,
42
Carriere, R.A., 40
Carruthers, J., 162
Carson, D., 71, 125
Carter-Oliver, C.C., 102

# INDEX

Carter's Nursing Home, 8
Case, K.I., 60, 125
Case Western Reserve University, 7
Castetter, W.B., 35, 37
Caswell County Training School, 129
Chapman, R.L., 158
Child Trends Data Bank, 70
Clarke, J.H., 10
class, 17–18
class culture, 18
Cleaver, K., 10
Coleman, J., xvi
Collins, P.H., 59, 68, 73
collusion, 146
Columbus, C., xvii
Combs, W.E., 157, 158
commitment, xxi, xxii, xxiii, xxiv, 32, 44–45,
    123–26, 128–29, 130, 131, 147, 153, 161,
    165–66
commitment to students, 105
communication facilitation, 160
compassion, xxi, xxii, xxiii, xxiv, 32, 45–47,
    123––26, 128–29, 130, 131, 147, 153,
    166, 165–66
Complexity Leadership Theory, 75
confidence, xxi, xxii, xxiii, xxiv, 32, 47, 123–26,
    128–29, 130, 131, 147, 153, 166, 165–66
control, 147
cooperation, 37
Coppin, F.J., 56, 96
corporal punishment, 18
Council of Independent Black Institutions
    (CIBI), xxii, 6, 8, 159, 160
counter-storytelling, 101
Craig, L.L., 73
Cramer, T.L., 107
Crenshaw, K., 69, 99, 100
Critical Race Theory (CRT), 57, 64, 66, 69,
    70, 74, 75, 77, 95, 99–101, 102, 103,
    104, 105, 106, 107, 108, 110, 111, 126,
    127, 130
    five tenets of, 101
    goal of, 101
critical self-reflection, 137, 150, 151, 152
Cuban, L., 12, 160
cultural collision, 146
cultural competence, 137–38
cultural differences, xvi, 140
cultural inclusion, xx
cultural womb, 67

culturally responsive pedagogy/teaching
    (CRP/T), xxii, xxiv, xxv, 9, 127, 142,
    145–46, 149–50, 153, 166
    assumptions about, 136–40
    early research on, 135–36
    ethno-humanism and, 135, 140, 141,
    166
    practice of, 151–52
    research and, 153
    six assumptions about, 166
    three Cs and, 141
    three foci of, 135–36
culturally responsive school leadership
    (CRSL), xx, xxii, xxiv–xxv, 63, 127,
    145–46, 153–54, 168
    community-based leadership and,
    148–49
    four critical pillars of, 150
    four dimensions of, 148
    importance of, 149–51
    practice of, 151–52
    principal preparation programs and,
    152
    research and, 153
    six themes of, 148
    three critical assumptions of, 150
    three levels of, 148
    understanding, 147–49
culture, 139
    education and, 138
    race and, 137
    seven components of, 17
Curriculum Integration Project (CIP), 34–35,
    35–43, 43–47

## D

Dade County Public Schools, 158
Dawson, N.C., 105, 126, 130
deficit analyses, 138
Delgado, R., 99
Derrick, L., 105
Dillard, C.B., 60, 125, 126, 129
Dillard, N.L., 129
Dixon, R.D., 168, 169
double consciousness, 73
Douglass, F., 170
Du Bois, W.E.B., 73
Duck, G.A., 40
Dunbar, J.N., 56, 96, 126, 127, 130
Duncan, A., 70
Durr, M., 74

# INDEX

**E**

Eagley, A.H., 59
Ebonics dialect, 138
Edmonds, R., 15, 170
education, 33–34, 163
    culture and, 138–39
    definition, 163
    schooling and, xviii–xx, 30, 49, 125,
       147, 178–79
Education Resources Information Center
    (ERIC), 98
*Educational Administration Quarterly,* 107
*Educational Researcher,* 55, 95
effective schools, 15
energy harnessing, 160
Erlandson, D.A., xxiii, 68
ethno-humanism, 165
    assessment of research on, 129–30
    culturally responsive pedagogy/
       teaching (CRP/T) and, 135, 140, 141,
       166
    principal preparation and, 177–78
    research on, 126–28, 128–29
    three Cs and, 130, 131, 141
ethno-humanist role identity, xx, xxi, xxii,
    xxiii, xxiv, xxv, xxvi, 29–30, 44–47,
    63, 145–46, 150, 161, 163
    Black male principals and, 107, 109,
       146–47
    commitment and, 44–45
    compassion and, 45–47
    confidence and, 47
Eubanks, S.C., 9
Eurasia, xvii
Ezzani, M., 148

**F**

Farrakhan, L., 10
Fine, M., 32, 34
Fortenberry, D.B., 62
Foster, M., 135, 138
Frederiksen, J., 15
Friday Night Lecture Series, 9
Funchess, M., 102, 103, 158

**G**

Gallien, E., xxiv
Gay, G., xxiv, 136, 138
genetic deficit, xvi
George Washington Carver Comprehensive
    High School, 129
Georgia State University, 11

Gillbord, D., 69
Gintis, H., xvi, 32
Giovanni, N., 10
goal development, 160
*Going to School: The African-American
    Experience,* xii
Gooden, M., xxiv, 126, 127, 130, 146, 161
Gordon, S.P., 148, 150, 152, 153
Gotada, N., 69
Greenleigh Associates, 20
Grubbs, C., 102, 103

**H**

Hale-Benson, J., xvi
Haslam, S.A., 74
Hatton, B., 11
Haynes, A.M., 73
Heidi, M., 57
Henderson, G.D., xxiv, 106, 126, 127, 128,
    130, 139
Herndon, J.D., 59
Hill, K.G., 32
Hines, S.A., 159
Hinton, K., 129
historically Black colleges and universities
    (HBCUs), 168
Hobson-Horton, L., 60, 73
Holbert, M., 9
Holzman, M., 57
homophily, 19, 20, 33, 58
hooks, b., 59, 68
Horsford, S.D., 62, 148, 153
Horton, P., 18
Howard, A., 149
Howard, T.C., 58, 137
Human Motivational Needs, 101
Humphrey, D.L., 104
Hunt, C., 18

**I**

institutionalized White racism, 69, 70
institutionalized White supremacy, xv,
    xviii, 99, 100, 101, 102, 150, 154, 157,
    162–64, 165, 169
instructional leadership, 160
*Integrated Education,* 158
interest convergency, 101

**J**

Jackson, J., 10
Jackson, S., 104
Jacobson, S., 76

# INDEX

187

Jean-Marie, G., xxiii, 73
Jensen, A., xvi
Jochannon, Y.b., 10
Johnson, B.T., 59
Johnson, C., 103, 104
Johnson, L., 58, 145, 148, 153
Johnson, S.O., 159
Jones, U., 8, 9
*Journal of Negro Education, The*, 158

### K

Karenga, M., 10, 17, 34
Keeves, G.D., 74
Kelley, G.J., 58, 139
Khalifa, M.A., xx, xxiv, 126, 129, 145, 148, 149,
    150, 153
King, C., 76
King, D.K., 73
King, J., 11
Kirst, M., 160
Kochman, T., 19, 58

### L

Ladson-Billings, G., xvi, xxiv, 69, 100, 135,
    136, 140
Leader-Member Exchange Theory, 101, 106
Leadership for Social Justice, 75
Leathers, S., 73
Lee, R., 58
Lezotte, L., 16, 42, 147
liberalism, 69, 101
Lightfoot, S.L., 126, 129
Lived Experiences, 105
Loder, T.L., 62, 125
Loeb, S., 58
Lomotey, Juba, 11
Lomotey, Kofi, xv, xvi, xvii, xix, xx, xxi, xxiii,
    xxv, 5, 9, 19, 20, 21, 22, 23, 29, 30, 32,
    34, 35, 43, 55, 58, 60, 76, 98, 100, 101,
    125, 126, 139, 147, 150, 159, 161, 162,
    175, 176, 177, 179
    background of, xi–xii
    birth of, 1
    death of father, 2
    death of grandfather, 2
    early career of, 3–4
    early years of life, 1–2
    education of, 2–3, 4–8, 9–10
    five recommendations for practice of
    Black principals, 167
    launching of African-centered
    school, 7–9, 159–60

marriage to Aama Nahuja, 4
at Oberlin College, xi, xxii, 4, 5, 6,
    160–61
at Stanford University, xi, xxii, 10,
    160–61
travel to Ghana and Nigeria, 6–7
travel to People's Republic of China,
    7
Lopez, A.E., 148, 150, 153
Louis, K.S., 37
Loveless, T., 70
Lowery, K., 161
Lyman, L., 126, 129
Lynn, M., 100
Lythcott, M., 4

### M

Mack, Y.S., 71
MacLennan, B.W., 19, 58
MacQueen, A.H., 40
Madhubuti, H., 10, 148, 150, 153
Mahoney, A.D., 147, 153
Marie, D.L.H., 31
Marion, R., 75
Marshall, M., 22
Marshall, S.L., 145
Masci, D., 67, 68
Mayienga, D.M., 62
McCray, C., xxiv, 146
McDonald, M.L., 74
McDonough, B., 62, 98
McGregor, D., 37
McKelvey, B., 75
McLaughlin, M., 12
mentoring, 76
Mercator projection, xviii
Miles, M.B., 37
Miller, M.A., 104, 105, 106
Milner, H.R., 58, 150
Mitchell, C., 62
Monteiro, T., 21
Moultry, E.G., 102, 103
Murnane, R. J., 20
Murrell, P.C., 58

### N

Nahuja, Aama, 4, 10
Nathan, G., 129
National Assessment of Education Progress,
    176
National Center for Education Statistics
    (NCES), 175, 176

## INDEX

National Center for Educational Studies, 58
Newcolm, W., 71
Nkrumah, K., 9
Nobles, W.W., xvii, 162

### O

Oberlin College, xi, xxii, 4, 5, 6, 160–61
Oberlin High School, 5
Ogbu, J., xvi
opportunity gap, xvi
Oreskovic, T., 98

### P

Page, S.W., 63
Palija, L., 105, 106
Parker, L., 100
Parker, W.S. Jr., 22
Patterson, J., 58, 60, 126, 129, 139
Payne, H.D., 4, 7, 9
Peek, B., 4–6
Peller, G., 69
Peter Stuyvesant High School, 3
Pickney, A., 17
power, xvii
Pressley, D., 129
Prichard, K., 158
principal preparation programs (PPPs), 168
Public School 123, xi
Putnam, R.D., 139

### R

race/racism, 17, 100, 102, 157, 176
    culture and, 137
race culture, 18
radical care framework, 107, 128
Reed, L.C., xxiii, 73
Reitzug, U.C., 58, 60, 126, 129, 139
Research on the Leadership of Black Women
    Principals, xxiv
Resilience Theory, 101, 104
Richardson, R.E., 108
Rist, R., 16, 158, 159
Rivera-McClutchen, R.L., 106, 107, 126, 128,
    130
Roan, T., 71
Robbins, L.C., 125
Rogers, E.M., 19, 33, 58
roles, 32–33
Ronder, E.A., 152
Ryan, M.K., 74

### S

Saaka, Y., 4, 6–7
Sanchez, S., 10
Satterwhite, F. See O. Babalawo
Scheurich, J., xxvi
schooling, 33
    definition, 163
    education and, xviii–xx, 30, 49, 125,
        147, 163, 178–79
Scott, J., 125
Seashore, K., xxv–xxvi
Self-Efficacy Theory, 101, 108
self-reflection, 139, 153
Sherman, S.L., 73
Shields, C.M., 75
Shockley, K., 162
Shoemaker, F.F., 19, 33, 58
Shorter-Gooden, K., 59, 73
Shujaa, K.J., 66
Shujaa, M., xiii, xix, 30, 33, 34, 66, 125, 130,
        147, 163, 164, 165
Shule ya Kujitambua, 8–9, 160
Shule Ya Taifa, 12
Siddle Walker, V., 107, 126, 129, 149
Smith, J., 102, 103, 106, 107
Smith, P.A., 102, 103
Smith, S., 56, 57, 96
social deficit, xvi
Sowell, T., 18, 19
Spady, W., 20
Spicer, Y.M., 66, 68
spirituality, 64, 66–68, 76
Spring, J., xvii
Springfield Gardens High School, 3
Staley, J., 31
Standard English, 138
Standpoint Theory (ST), 57, 64, 66, 68–70,
        74, 75
Stanford University, xi, xxii, 10, 160–61
Stefanic, J., 99
Stewart, B., 98
structural inequalities, xvi
Stryker, S., 33

### T

Taliaferro, A., 150
Tate, W., 100
teacher-to-principal pipeline, 104
Teichert, L., 31
Thomas, K., 69
Thomas, M.J., 102, 103

# INDEX

189

three Cs, xxi, xxii, xxiii, xxiv, 32, 44–45,
123–26, 128–29, 130, 131, 145, 147, 153,
161, 165–66
Tillman, L., xxiv, 55, 56, 58, 72, 96, 126, 128,
129, 139, 146, 161
transformational leadership, 63
Transformative Leadership Theory, 74, 101,
104, 109
Turbyfill, R.L., 97, 106, 107
Turner, C.T., 62
Turner, R.C., 107, 108
Tweedle, P.W.D., 60, 67
two-way communication, 40

## U

Uhl-Bien, M., 75
Uhuru Sasa Shule, 8, 160
University Council for Educational Administration (UCEA), xxvi
*Urban Education*, xxiii, xxiv
U.S. Equal Employment Opportunity
Commission, 55, 97

## V

Van Sertima, I., xvii, 10
Vargas, S.R., 146

## W

Washington, T., 105, 106
Watson, G., 2
Weaver, R., 9
Weaver, T.L., 126, 127, 130, 140, 147
Wellisch, J.B., 40, 42
Western Carolina University, 61, 97
Westphal, J.D., 74
Weusi, K.J., 8, 160
White male principals
leadership of, 60
White privilege, 102
White supremacy, xv
Whiteness, 101
Wilkerson, R.D., 128, 130
Williams, I., 58, 139
Williams, V.A., 73
Wilson, A., xvi
Wilson, E.E., 128, 130
Wilson, W.J., 17
Wingfield, A.M.H., 74
wolf ticket, 2
worldview, 162